The New Business Letter Writer

The New Business Letter Writer

Edited by **Derek Hall**

W. Foulsham & Co. Ltd.

London · New York · Toronto · Cape Town · Sydney

W. Foulsham & Company Limited
Yeovil Road, Slough, Berkshire, SL1 4JH

ISBN 0-572-01333-7

The publishers would like to point out that all the names of people,
companies, publications, trade goods, etc., as well as all the addresses to
be found in this book, are intended to be entirely fictional. Any similarities
with actual names are entirely coincidental.

Printed in Great Britain
by St Edmundsbury Press,
Bury St Edmunds, Suffolk

CONTENTS

INTRODUCTION

All of us have to write 'business' letters at some time or another. You may need to include a covering letter with a job application, or want to ask your bank manager for an overdraft. You may run a retail business and need to order supplies from a wholesaler, or you may wish to write to potential customers to try and persuade them to buy your goods or services.

You, and your business, will be judged by the letters you send, and this book provides a basic grounding in business letter writing to help you produce effective, well-presented letters. It is aimed in particular at individuals and small or new businesses, although people in larger, long-established firms may still find much of help and interest. The first part of the book begins by outlining points you should keep in mind while writing business letters, the choice of stationery, and whether, in fact, a letter is the most appropriate means of communication for your particular needs; it also deals with the main layout styles and the standard parts of a typical letter. This is followed by advice on the practicalities of writing a letter, including effective dictation, typing, copying and filing; mention is also made of some of the recent advances in office technology to help you decide whether machines such as a word processor would help you in your business letter writing.

The letters given as examples in the second part of this book are grouped into broad subject areas. You are unlikely to find exactly the letter you need for your purpose in every case, but hopefully the examples will provide guidance as to the correct tone and style to adopt, and a framework on which to base a letter. Indeed, your letters should be an expression of you (and your business), so you will want to make some changes in order to inject some of your own personality into them. The letter examples given here are, of course, all imaginary, as are the names and addresses used. The letters do not include those of a strictly 'legal' nature which may need to be cited in litigation. Here the exact wording is important, and if you have such a letter to write you would be well advised to seek professional advice.

Finally, there are appendices which deal with such topics as basic points of grammar and commonly misspelled words.

Useful points to remember

1 The aim of the letter: despite the variety of topics on which business letters are written, they all have at least one of three purposes: to convey information; to prompt action; or to maintain a satisfactory working relationship. The purpose is likely to affect the tone and style of your letter, so it is important to keep the general, as well as your more specific, aim in mind.

2 The person to whom you are writing: anything you know about your correspondent or their business can help you write a more effective letter. Try to put yourself in your correspondent's shoes and you may be able to judge how he or she is likely to react; this may suggest ways in which you can improve your letter.

3 Clarity of thought and expression: the importance of organising your thoughts and noting down the main points before writing or replying to a letter is stressed throughout this book. It is also important that, having decided what you want to say, you express yourself in a way the recipient will understand. Try to use short words and short sentences which convey the message simply and clearly. Long words and complex grammatical constructions are more difficult to read and are often imprecise. If you do sometimes use long words — and they cannot always be avoided — get into the habit of checking their meaning and spelling in a dictionary. It is surprising how often they do not convey quite the meaning you intended. Similarly, try not to use too much technical jargon, and avoid 'foreign' phrases where there is a straightforward English equivalent; you want the recipient to understand your letter, not to marvel at your knowledge. Some long or complex words and phrases and shorter, simpler alternatives are given in Appendix A at the back of the book, together with a brief summary of English usage: grammar, punctuation, spelling, etc.

4 Clichés and 'commercial letter phrases': avoid phrases such as 'Permit me to state' or 'We beg to acknowledge receipt of your letter'. These are clichés, and usually add little or nothing to your meaning. The first example could be dispensed with altogether — just go ahead and state; the second would be better written 'Thank you for your letter'. Try and think how you would express an idea if you were talking face to face with the person; this is often a good guide to avoiding 'commercialesé, since few people would actually say 'Permit me to state'. Some of the most common business clichés and their possible alternatives are given in Appendix B.

5 Courtesy and honesty: these qualities are important in a letter not merely because they are the correct way to behave, but also because you are committing yourself to paper. If you write anything libellous, for example, you may well end up in court. Remember it is not only the person you are writing to who may read the letter. If you are writing a letter of complaint, think very carefully before choosing your words. Try not to be abusive, but if you simply must get it off your chest, then write it and sleep on it. In the morning you will probably prefer to throw that particular letter away rather than send it.

6 Accuracy and completeness: always date the letter and check that the recipient's name and address are given correctly. Read the letter over before sealing it, especially if someone has typed the letter for you. Check spelling, punctuation and grammar, any facts and figures and if enclosures are mentioned make sure that they really are there. Finally make sure you put the letter in the correct envelope.

Stationery

Business notepaper should be of good quality. Paper suitable for letters often goes under names including the words 'Bond', 'Script', etc, and is classified according to its weight. A weight of about 70-90 grams per square metre (g/m^2) is suitable for most purposes. Most business letters are written on plain white paper but sometimes plain pastel colours are used and, especially if teamed with a suitable letterheading, may be more in keeping with the desired business image.

Paper of A4 size (210 × 297 mm/$8\frac{1}{4}$ × $11\frac{3}{4}$ inches) is generally most satisfactory, giving adequate space for most letters, but a stock of A5 paper (which is half the size of A4 — see diagram) may be useful for shorter letters. A5 paper can be used either with its longer side from top to bottom (portrait style) or with the longer dimension running from side to side (landscape style). Other paper sizes based on imperial measurements such as foolscap (8 × 13 inches), quarto (8 × 10 inches) and octavo (5 × 8 inches) may still have particular applications in certain businesses, but they have now largely been superseded by the internationally standardised A series.

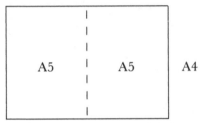

One sheet of A4 paper can be divided into two sheets of A5.

Nearly all businesses, as well as many private individuals, have a printed letterheading on their notepaper. Like all the other parts of the letter the letterheading should present a suitable image, so it is worth spending some time, and perhaps seeking expert help, to devise a good letterheading. All businesses will obviously need to include the business name, address and telephone number, but it may also be useful to include a brief description of the type of business — eg R Johnson & Sons (Builders) — if this is not apparent from the business name. Partnerships and registered companies are also required by law to include certain other details such as the company registration number and the registered office address, and businesses with telegraphic addresses or telexes would, of course, also include these details in their letterheading. Don't forget when ordering headed notepaper that you will almost certainly need some continuation sheets; these should match the printed paper in size, weight and colour, and are best purchased at the same time.

Envelopes, likewise, should ideally match the paper, although some businesses use manilla envelopes for all their correspondence, and for long letters consisting of several sheets or for letters enclosing booklets, etc, the strength of the envelope may be more important than a match. It is possible to have your business name and address printed on the envelopes, too, and, as well as providing publicity, this also has the advantage that undelivered mail can be returned to you. Such details are usually printed at the top left of the envelope and should match the printed letterheading in style, although they will usually be much smaller. A business address may also be included in a special frank if you hire a franking machine.

A series of envelope sizes has been developed which relates to the international paper sizes. The envelope sizes are prefixed by C, and will take an unfolded sheet of the equivalently numbered paper. Therefore a C4 envelope will take an unfolded sheet of A4; a C5 envelope an unfolded sheet of A5 (or A4 paper folded in half); and a C6 envelope will take an unfolded sheet of A6 (or A5 paper folded in half, or A4 paper folded into quarters). C6 envelopes are suitable for most normal correspondence, with C4 and C5 sizes more appropriate for longer letters. As with paper, other traditional sizes of envelopes are still available, and one that is particularly useful for business correspondence is known as DL. DL envelopes are 110×220 mm ($4\frac{1}{4} \times 8\frac{5}{8}$ inches) and will take A4 paper folded into thirds.

Other methods of communication

The telephone

Studies have shown that by the time all the costs of producing a letter (the writer's time, the typist's time, stationery costs, etc) are added up it is frequently cheaper to make a phone call. This is especially so for local calls but often applies to longer distance calls as well. A phone call has the advantages that it demands attention (it's much easier to ignore a letter than a ringing phone!), produces an immediate reply and enables problems and misunderstandings to be cleared up on the spot.

However, some of the advantages of letters include the fact that they provide a complete written record for future reference, they are often better than a phone call if something upsetting or sensitive needs to be said, they are more easily understood than the spoken word by people communicating in a foreign language, and a reply can be planned (and/or discussed with colleagues) whereas with a telephone you tend to give an instant, and perhaps not fully considered, response.

In many cases a combination of letter and phone call is appropriate. For example you might make a booking for a hotel by phone (when you can enquire about vacancies, suitable facilities, costs, etc), and then confirm the booking by letter. Or perhaps if you are selling goods or services you may send a letter to introduce your business to a potential customer. You can then follow this up by a phone call with which you hope to make an appointment to take things further.

Telex and teletex

The telex system uses teleprinters to send messages rapidly between subscribers, and operates internationally. Teletex is a recent update which provides more rapid transmission and will become part of an integrated electronic mail service where messages can be stored, edited and retrieved in the same way as other computerised information. The message is typed on to a machine which has a typewriter-like keyboard (though telex uses capital letters and figures only), is transmitted to the recipient by a special network, and is automatically typed out on the recipient's machine. An alarm bell on the recipient's machine may warn them that a message has been received. Telex has the advantages of a letter in that the message is planned in advance and a permanent record of what was sent can be obtained, and like the telephone it has the advantage of speed. Also, as it is a 24-hour service, it is useful for sending messages to countries in different time zones, since the message can arrive on their teleprinter overnight, ready for attention first thing the following morning. The main disadvantage is that telex can only be used for communications between two subscribers: however, some office service businesses have machines available for their clients' use.

Telemessages and telegrams

Telemessages provide a 24-hour service within the UK and between the UK and the USA, and are useful if you want to send reasonably short letters or messages more quickly than is possible using the standard postal services. Telemessages received up to 10 pm Monday to Saturday will be delivered during the next working day, so they are particularly useful after normal office hours.

Telemessages are charged in 50-word units (excluding the sender's and recipient's addresses) with subsequent units being cheaper than the first. The maximum length is approximately 350 words (about the same as a letter typed single-spaced on a sheet of A4 paper).

Telemessages can be sent via the telephone (by phoning 100, or 190 in London) or via the telex service, and in Britain these are then routed via British Telecom's computer data network to a receiving terminal near to the destination. The message is then printed out ready for local delivery. For a small additional charge the sender can receive a confirmation copy. It is also possible to send multiple telemessages from a single call, and British Telecom will store a list of recipients for you if you regularly send telemessages to the same group of people.

International telegrams are a similar system whereby short messages can be sent to addresses worldwide. It is also a 24-hour service, with messages being registered via telephone or telex. As with the old telegram service within the UK (which telemessages have now replaced), the charge is based on the number of words. It is therefore important to plan your telegrams carefully in advance in order to be concise without being ambiguous.

Postcards

Postcards are usually no quicker or cheaper than letters, but are sometimes useful for acknowledgements or other standard and brief correspondence. Cards may be printed with a name and address, and may also be printed with a standard message with spaces for the date, any necessary reference numbers, etc. However, used in such a way they are a rather impersonal form of communication, and they are also open for anyone to read; these aspects should be considered when deciding whether to use a postcard. The opening greeting and complimentary close are generally omitted on postcards and the recipient's address should not be repeated on the message side.

Memoranda

Memoranda are used for inter-office communications where an ordinary letter would be inappropriate but where a written record is required. Many businesses have preprinted forms (on A5 landscape paper) with spaces for the details of sender and recipient, date, reference, the subject of the memorandum and the message itself. If plain paper is used all these details should be included. The recipient's address, opening greeting and complimentary close are usually omitted, and the sender usually just initials rather than signs the memo.

Facsimile transmission (fax)

There are various services available whereby copies of documents, including pictorial matter such as maps and diagrams, can be transmitted rapidly both within a country and overseas. The documents usually have to be taken to and collected from large central offices (although in Britain a messenger service is also available) and this tends to limit its use to businesses in or near large towns and cities. There are also limits on the size of document that can be transmitted. However, it is also possible to send information to or from facsimile machines based at a customer's business premises, although the equipment will not be cheap. Main post offices and British Telecom should be able to provide details of the services available in Britain.

Computer networks

With recent developments in computer technology there are now a number of ways in which messages can be sent from one computer terminal to another, usually via telephone connections, and interactive communication is also possible with suitably compatible equipment. This will no doubt be a growing form of communication with the advantages of both the immediacy of telephones and the permanency of letters (as long as a print-out is obtained), but the hardware necessary to communicate in this way is still relatively expensive and not available as yet to many individuals or small businesses.

LAYOUT AND STYLE

Although there is no one correct way to lay out a business letter, it is important to develop an attractive and consistent style. The remainder of this section outlines the main styles used in business letters and then describes the individual parts of the letter.

The fully blocked, semi-blocked and indented styles

The two styles of letter layout usually used in business correspondence are known as fully blocked (or just blocked) and semi-blocked (sometimes also referred to as indented). They differ mainly in whether or not the paragraphs are indented, in the position of the date, any subject heading, and the complimentary close: Examples 1 and 2 show and detail these differences. The fully blocked style tends to give a more 'modern' look to a letter, but both styles are equally correct. However, they should not be mixed within a letter and, ideally, one or the other should be used for all your business correspondence to promote a consistent image of the business.

The true indented style differs from semi-blocked in having the sender's address and the complimentary close 'stepped', ie each line is indented a couple of spaces more than the one above. It is more appropriate for personal than for business correspondence.

Punctuation styles — open and closed punctuation

The other main choice to be made in developing a house style for letters concerns the use of punctuation, especially in the peripheral parts of the letter. Open punctuation involves minimal punctuation and is the method normally used with the fully blocked style, as in Example 1. In closed punctuation — also known as traditional or full punctuation — commas are used after the address lines and after the opening greeting and complimentary close. This style is shown in Example 2, together with the semi-blocked layout.

Example 1 Fully blocked and open punctuation styles

42 Botley Close
Colebourn
RIPON
Yorks
R18 7QS

Your ref 5/12A

17 May 19 -

Messrs Brown & Page (Builders)
28A Long Lane
RIPON
Yorks
R12 1AN

Dear Sirs

QUOTATION FOR EXTENSION AT 42 BOTLEY CLOSE

Thank you for your estimate dated 5 May 19 -.

I am sorry to have to tell you, however, that the figure quoted is in excess of others that we have received and we shall therefore not be pursuing the matter further with you.

Thank you for supplying the quotation, nevertheless.

Yours faithfully

John Smith

John Smith

Blocked: Date,* subject heading, complimentary close and any displayed matter all to the left margin. No indentations for paragraphs. Capital letters usually used for 'for attention lines' and subject headings.

*The date is sometimes placed in line with the sender's address on the right-hand side; this makes it easier to find in files.

Open punctuation: No punctuation used outside the main body of the letter unless essential for sense (eg if both a town and a county in an address are put on the same line they should be separated by a comma or two spaces). Use numbers without -th endings in dates and no fullstops in any abbreviations, contractions or acronyms (eg Mr J Jones, NATO, BSc or MP).

Example 2 Semi-blocked and closed punctuation styles

42 Botley Close,
Colebourn,
RIPON,
Yorks.
R18 7QS

Your ref: 5/12A   17th May 19 -

Messrs Brown & Page (Builders),
28A Long Lane,
RIPON,
Yorks.
R12 1AN

Dear Sirs,

<u>Quotation for extension at 42 Botley Close</u>

Thank you for your estimate dated 5th May 19 -.

I am sorry to have to tell you, however, that the figure quoted is in excess of others that we have received and we shall therefore not be pursuing the matter further with you.

Thank you for supplying the quotation, nevertheless.

Yours faithfully,

John Smith

John Smith

Semi-blocked: Date to right-hand side, aligned with sender's address if typed, and on the same line as any reference code. Subject heading, complimentary close and any displayed matter all centred. Indentation for first lines of paragraphs.

Closed punctuation: Commas after each line of the addresses and after the opening greeting and complimentary close. Numbers used with -th endings in dates. Full stops in abbreviations but not usually in contractions or acronyms, (eg Mr J. Jones, NATO, B.Sc. or M.P.).

The basic framework of a letter

Although business letters deal with a wide range of topics, it is possible to categorise the main parts of a typical letter. This is done in Example 3. Most letters would not contain all these features, but they should all contain the essential parts, namely: a business/sender's address, a date, a recipient's name and address, an opening greeting, the main body of the letter, a complimentary close, a signature and a sender's name.

The business name

Any business name should be typed above the address. Abbreviations such as the ampersand (&), Co, Ltd, plc or PLC, are usual in such names. However, business names and addresses are in most cases already included as part of the printed letterheading.

The business/sender's address

Unless a business is very small, or newly formed, this address will probably be part of the printed letterheading. However, whether printed or typed, the full postal address (including the country if much foreign correspondence is envisaged) should be used so that the recipient knows exactly where to reply. Guidance as to what to include is given in the section on the recipient's address, and your local post office will also be able to tell you your correct postal address and post code if you are not sure of these.

A telephone number, giving the exchange name (and possibly also the STD code), should be included if this is likely to be an appropriate and acceptable form of reply for the recipient to use. (On headed notepaper a logo, a telegraphic address, a telex number, etc, may also be included.)

In both the fully blocked and semi-blocked styles the sender's name and address is usually typed at the top right of a letter, aligned on the longest line, or for the semi-blocked style each line can be centred on the paper.

Example 3 The parts of a letter

Business name
Business/sender's address
(usually replaced by a
printed letterheading)

Reference code

Date

CLASSIFICATION

TYPE OF POSTAL SERVICE

Recipient's name
Recipient's address

FOR THE ATTENTION OF

Opening greeting

SUBJECT HEADING

Main body of letter. Xxxxx xx xxxxxxxx xxx xx xx xxxx xxx. Xx
xxx xxxxxx xx x xxxx xx xxxxx.

Xxxx xxxxxx x xxxx xx xxxxxx x xxxx xxxxxxxx xxx   xx xx xxxx.
Xxx xxx xxxxxx xx xxxxx xx xxx xx xxxxx.

Complimentary close
Company name

Sender's name
Sender's position/department name

Enclosures line

Copies line

Reference code
Reference codes are used on letters to help in filing or to indicate the
names of the people writing and typing the letter (eg BJE/glm). However,
letters are often filed according to the recipient's name or organisation

(which is already included in the rest of the letter), and there is no point in adding a reference code just to make the letter look more 'business-like'.

The reference code is usually given in the form 'Ref _____', 'Ref: _____' or 'Ref. _____' at the top left of the letter. If your correspondent quotes a reference code your reply should include that too, ie Our ref: _____

Your ref: _____

Date

The date should always be given in full and not in the form of numbers such as 8.2.19——. This is because in Britain the day tends to be given first whereas in the United States the month is usually given first. Therefore 8.2.19—— could be read as 8 February or 2 August! It is also much clearer not to abbreviate month names or years, and the year should always be included as it may be important in referring back to past correspondence for both you and the recipient. Avoid using 'Date as postmark' as the envelope is usually soon discarded, and neither you nor your correspondent will probably remember when it was sent. The most common forms for the date (in the UK) are 8 February 19—— and 8th February 19——. The endings -th, -nd, etc, are appropriate to the closed style of punctuation, and in closed punctuation a comma may also be used before the year.

Classification line

If your letter is personal or confidential, this may be indicated at the top left of the letter. Use 'PERSONAL' if the letter must be opened by the recipient only; a 'CONFIDENTIAL' letter may be opened by his or her deputy but should, of course, still be treated confidentially. The words are usually typed in capital letters and/or underlined. This information as to the type of letter should also be repeated on the envelope.

Type of postal service to be used

Sometimes it may be useful to indicate the type of postal service to be used for a letter (eg 'Recorded Delivery', 'Registered Post', 'Airmail'). This is usually typed in capitals at the top left of the letter, or a sticky label may be used instead.

Recipient's name

If possible you should include the name of an individual recipient or at least a specific job title. This makes the letter someone's particular responsibility and hopefully leads to a quicker reply. It may also be useful if you need to follow up the letter and want to know to whom you wrote in the past. However, as an alternative the name of a department plus the organisation's name, or just the organisation, may be given here. Sometimes a letter may say 'All communications should be addressed to _____' and in this case you should obviously follow instructions.

An individual's name As a guide to use of first names and/or initials you should follow the writer's preferred style as indicated by past correspondence. There should always be a courtesy title, and the spellings of names should be carefully copied.

The most common courtesy titles are Mr, Mrs, Miss or Ms. Esq, which indicated the status of 'gentleman' in the past, may be used instead of Mr but *not* with it (ie either Mr J Brown of J Brown, Esq). However, Esq can only be used if you know the first name(s) or initial(s) and Mr is probably the best courtesy title to use for most male correspondents.

If a woman has indicated on past correspondence her preferred courtesy title you should use this. If not, and you are unsure as to her marital status, it is generally acceptable to use either Ms or Miss. Most women nowadays prefer their own (rather than their husband's) first name(s) or initial(s) to be used, and her names or initials should certainly be used if she is known to be widowed or separated. If a married woman uses her maiden name the courtesy title Miss or Ms is used.

Other courtesy titles are related to qualifications, professions or honours. They replace the normal courtesy titles, and only very occasionally is it correct to use more than one courtesy title; an example where two courtesy titles is correct is Admiral Sir _____.

Dr or Doctor can be used for a man or a woman, and is used if the person has a doctoral degree as well as for medical doctors. (However, surgeons are traditionally addressed as Mr!). Don't use both Dr and MD.

Clergymen should be addressed as 'The Rev J (or John) Smith' and not just as 'Rev Smith'.

Knight's names should always include their first name (not initial) and surname (eg Sir John Price not Sir J Price).

There are also recognised ways of addressing titled persons, and these together with the appropriate opening greetings and complimentary closes are given in Appendix C of this book.

Sometimes letters denoting honours, qualifications or professions may be used after the name, and there are accepted rules for the order in which these should be given. If a person has a number of 'letters' it is usual to use only one or two of the most high-ranking ones, and university degrees or professional qualifications are not usually included unless they are particularly relevant (eg you may add ARIBA to an architect's name when writing to him in his professional capacity, but you would be unlikely to add BSc to your landlord's name just because you know he had a degree).

The accepted order for letters is as follows: order of chivalry (eg OBE) — highest first (but a higher grade of a junior order precedes a lower grade of a senior order); decorations (eg VC) — highest first; crown appointments (eg JP); university degrees — lowest first (eg BSc, MA); professional qualifications (eg ARIBA); profession (eg MP, RN).

If there is likely to be any confusion between a father and son with the same names the abbreviation Jun or Jnr may be added to the younger person's name. It is less usual to add Snr for the older person.

Letters to more than one individual usually use the courtesy titles Mr and Mrs (or Dr and Mrs, or Mr and Dr) plus the man's name or initials and surname for a married couple; Messrs for two men; The Misses for two unmarried ladies; and Mesdames for two married ladies.

A job title or a department name In both these cases an organisation name should also be included as part of the address.

An organisation In most cases the organisation's name should be given in the version used in your correspondent's letterheading (eg A K Hunt & Sons Ltd). In the case of partnership the form 'Messrs Price & Greenwood' is correct.

Recipient's address

This should be copied carefully from the previous correspondence if available and should be the same as the address to be used on the envelope. Avoid using abbreviations for road or town names, although it is acceptable to use the standard county abbreviations.
Addresses should include:

1   A house or building number (and a flat, chamber or office number if appropriate). No comma is needed after the number before the road name. Avoid using just a house name if possible, and do not use inverted commas round house names.
2   A road name.
3   Possibly a village name, or a district of a town if there are several streets of the same name is a town.
4   The postal town. This is the town where letters are sorted for local delivery. The post town name should be given in capital letters.
5   A county — unless the town is a major city or shares the name with the county (eg Gloucestershire should not follow Gloucester).
6   Postcode. This consists of two blocks, of letters and numbers, the first block indicating a major area of the postal town, the second identifying the address down to a group of 15 or so houses, or even in some cases an individual firm's offices. There should be no punctuation in postcodes.

Each of these parts of an address is normally given an individual line and they should be given in the order listed above. However, inside the letter the district and town names, or town and county names may share a line (separated by a comma or extra space), or, more commonly, the (large) town and postcode or county and postcode share a line (separated by between two and six spaces).

In foreign addresses both the postal town and the county are usually capitalised, and zip codes, etc, should always, of course, be included.

'For the attention of' line

This line, which is traditionally placed between the recipient's address and the opening greeting, is used when only the name of a department or organisation has previously been given for the recipient. The usual wording is 'For the attention of Mrs J King' (underlined with no fullstop) and an attention line should be used as an alternative to, not as well as, a recipient's name of job name. The 'attention' line can also be placed immediately before the recipient's department or organisation and in the fully blocked style is often typed in capital letters (not underlined).

Opening greeting (or salutation)

The form of salutation used should be related to the way the recipient's name has been given.

If the letter is addressed to an individual the greeting would normally be in the form 'Dear Mr Westwood', 'Dear Miss Jones', etc, (ie the courtesy title and surname, but no initials or first names). If the recipient is a good friend, though, it would be appropriate to use the form 'Dear Jack' or similar, and the form 'Dear Anne Jones' is occasionally used as slightly less formal than 'Dear Miss Jones' but more formal than 'Dear Anne'. In general the best guideline is to consider how you would address the individual in person and use that form.

Letters addressed to only one person who has been addressed by office rather than by name should start 'Dear Sir' or 'Dear Madam'. If the sex of the person concerned is unknown, 'Dear Sir' or 'Dear Sir/Madam' or 'Dear Sir or Madam' would be acceptable in most cases.

If a whole department or organisation is being addressed the salutation would be 'Dear Sirs' (unless you knew it to be entirely staffed by women when 'Dear Mesdames' should be used).

The greetings 'Sir(s)' or 'Gentlemen' on their own are occasionally used but they are rather formal for most correspondence.

Subject heading

It is often helpful to both the sender and the recipient to give a subject heading immediately after the opening greeting. It should be short and concise and should match that given by your correspondent if you are continuing discussion of the same topic. The subject heading may quote an important reference number (eg an insurance policy number). It should be underlined (or in the fully blocked style it is often typed in capital letters) and has no final fullstop (eg 'Sale of 57 Billings Road' or 'INSURANCE POLICY NUMBER ABC/156181').

The main body of a letter

Sometimes it is difficult to think of suitable words with which to start the letter. The following may perhaps suggest some ideas.

Thank you for your letter of —
In reply to your letter of —
I am sorry to tell you —
As requested —
We wish to remind you that —
Referring to your letter of —

I enclose —
Please —
I have to point out —
We have carefully considered —
I am writing to —
We recently wrote to you about —
You may be interested to hear —
I am sorry to inform you that —
We would like to know —
I am wondering if you could —
I wish to —
With reference to your letter of —
I am delighted to tell you that —
I know you will be sorry to hear that —
I wish to draw your attention to —

You should always refer to any previous correspondence in the first paragraph and also try to get to the point of the letter reasonably quickly.

If a letter is long and complicated it may be useful to number points or to use paragraph headings (capitals or underlining) although this will tend to make the letter look rather formalised. In any case it is best to start a paragraph with a 'topic sentence', introducing the subject of the paragraph, as this will help your reader to follow your train of thought. However, if the letter has more than one main subject it may be worth considering sending two separate letters as this will make it easier for both your recipient and you to consign them to the appropriate person and/or files.

It is best to try and make the final paragraph positive and to state what you hope the recipient will do. Also you should include a personal pronoun in final statements (eg 'I hope to hear from you soon' rather than 'Hoping to hear from you soon').

Try and avoid PSs in letters. If your letter has been well planned as suggested in the next section, last-minute thoughts and additions should be unnecessary.

Complimentary close
This should match the opening greeting. 'Yours sincerely' or 'Yours faithfully' will be appropriate in nearly all cases: 'Yours sincerely' where the individual is named, and 'Yours faithfully' where the salutation is 'Dear Sir' or similar.

Other complimentary closes sometimes used include: 'Faithfully yours' or 'Sincerely yours' (which tend to sound a bit pompous), 'Yours respectfully' (sometimes used at the close of long, report-like letters), Your obedient servant' (only used in certain official letters), and 'Yours truly' (which can be used instead of 'Yours faithfully' but is a bit more formal). 'Best wishes' or some other greeting may of course be more appropriate if you know your correspondent well and have addressed him as 'Dear Jack' or something similar.

Company name

This indicates that the letter is on behalf of the company as a whole, even though it has been written and signed by a certain individual. The business name should always be given here if the plural 'we' form has been used in the main body of the letter. The company name is placed on the line immediately following the complimentary close and is usually in the form 'G Jones & Co' or 'for G Jones & Co'. If the person signing is an authorised signatory of the business the form 'per pro' or 'pp G Jones & Co' may be used.

Signature

Letters will usually bear the signature of the writer; however, sometimes other conventions are followed. A partner signing for his firm, for example, should use the firm's name without adding his own name. Sometimes, also, a proxy signature may be necessary, for example when the writer is not available to sign urgent letters. In this case something on the lines of the following examples would probably be appropriate.

A. Jones	A. Jones	A. Jones
for Marketing Director	for F Reed	Secretary to Mr F Reed
	Marketing Director	

A firm's rubber stamp in place of a signature is generally regarded as rather discourteous. Even for circular letters it is usually possible to include a printed or duplicated signature.

Sender's name

Unless you are confident that your signature is readable, or it will be very familiar to your correspondent, it is as well to include your name immediately below the signature. This should match the signature in terms of use of first names or initials. If just initials are given the recipient will probably assume the writer is a man; in any case it is helpful if a woman adds Mrs, Miss or Ms to the name to show the style of address she prefers.

Sender's office or department

This should be added, if appropriate, on the line following the name.

Enclosures

The word 'Enc' (or 'Encs', 'Encs — ', or 'Enc: Leaflet — ') is useful both to remind you to check that all enclosures are included, and to remind the recipient that enclosures are present. Sometimes a small coloured 'enclosures' label is used instead. Another way of indicating enclosures is to type a sign in the left margin of the letter opposite the point of mention. The signs commonly used are * ... . . . or /.

Copies line

If a letter is written to a certain person but is sent for information to others, it is helpful to all concerned to indicate who has been sent copies

by using wording such as 'Copies to Mr J Edwards
                                                    Mrs H Richards'
The copy for each individual can be marked by a tick against the name to
save any confusion when sending the letters out.

If you do not wish the recipient to know who has received carbon copies
'blind carbon copies' would be used with 'bcc Mr J Edwards', etc, being
typed on the carbons only.

Addressing envelopes

The envelope provides the first impression of your letter so it is important
that it should be neatly typed. The wording of the address should be as
given in the letter. The normal convention is to type the address length-
wise along the envelope, leaving the opening in long envelopes to the left.
The address should start about half-way down the envelope, leaving at
least 40 mm ($1\frac{1}{2}$ inches) or so above for the stamp and postal frank.

The post town should be given in capitals and all the parts of the
address should have separate lines as this makes it easier for the postal
services to deal with the letter quickly and efficiently, especially where
mechanised sorting is used. The postcode should always be the final line.
Any classification such as 'PERSONAL', 'CONFIDENTIAL', etc,
should be indicated on the envelope (a couple of lines above the name and
address) and you should also indicate (by typing or using sticky labels at
the top left of the envelope) the postal service to be used (First Class,
Recorded Delivery, Airmail, etc) especially if the letter will be posted by
someone else or dealt with in a mail department. With larger envelopes
and packages, which tend to be more prone to damage in the post, it is
particularly important to include the sender's address both on the outside
and inside of the package so that it can be returned if necessary — for
example if the recipient's address label comes off or becomes unreadable.
The sender's address should be clearly differentiated from the recipient's
address by its position and size and/or using the word 'From'.

BUSINESS LETTER WRITING PROCEDURES

Incoming mail

An efficient system for dealing with business correspondence starts with a suitable method of handling the incoming post. Open envelopes carefully — a letter knife helps here — and check that everything that should be enclosed *is* there. Note anything which seems to be missing so that this can be followed up. If there are several sheets it may be useful to clip them together to prevent them from becoming separated, and it may also be worth noting the date of receipt on the letter — especially if this is some time after the date it was sent or if the letter is undated.

The correspondence can then be read and sorted into categories: for example, for information only (which can go straight into your filing system); needing immediate attention; needing a reply but not quite so urgent, etc. The system adopted will obviously depend on the type and quantity of correspondence you receive.

Planning a letter

It is usually best to put aside certain times for writing letters as this is a job that otherwise often gets ignored until the pile of letters needing replies gets even larger and more discouraging. Most letters should be answered as promptly as possible as this indicates that both you and your business are efficient. However, some difficult letters will need much thought on your part or a discussion with colleagues, and these should not be rushed; however, once decisions have been made these letters, too, should be answered as promptly as possible. Also letters of complaint are sometimes best considered for a day or two; you may in retrospect be thankful that you did not commit your immediate thoughts to the post!

Once you are ready to write a letter assemble all the information you need. This will include any previous correspondence and perhaps items such as a sales brochure if you have a customer enquiry, or accounts sheets if you have a money query, and the standard form letter file (see below) if it appears to be a routine type of letter. Read any letters to be answered carefully, so that you are sure what is being asked.

For all but the shortest of business letters it is worth making a list of notes of the main points to be covered. These can then be worked into a logical order — which will help your correspondent follow the sense of your letter more easily. If some points seem repetitive or irrelevant, be ruthless and cross them out. You may then with to expand the basic framework. These notes can then serve as prompts for dictation, and even if you are drafting your letters in longhand or typing them yourself they will probably save you needing to make several attempts as you will have a logical framework to follow.

The rest of this section assumes that you will either be dictating to, or preparing a longhand draft for, a typist, or typing the letter yourself. However, if you are an individual writing letters on business subjects it would be acceptable to write in longhand (in black or blue ink), and this would probably look better than a poorly typed letter; however, even from an individual a well-typed letter would look best of all.

Printed or duplicated letters and standard form letter files

If you deal with a lot of similar correspondence it may be worth having a printed or duplicated answer letter, and/or a standard form letter file which contains examples of commonly used phrases or paragraphs.

Printed or duplicated letters are only really appropriate for routine replies such as sending out price lists and acknowledging orders or enquiries where the lack of the personal touch does not matter greatly. As well as the normal letterheading such letters would be printed with a short message, with space left for variables such as the date, recipient's name and address, reference code and signature. A typical example is shown in Example 4.

The design of such letters should be simple and the wording should be carefully thought out to make sure that the letter will not go out of date quickly. Also, when designing such a letter, take a copy of the proposed design and fill in the spaces with typical names, dates, etc, to make sure that sufficient space has been left!

Circular letters are a similar type of letter and are used where the same information needs to be sent to a number of people (eg members of a club or society or a firm's customers). They are usually generalised, and use opening greetings such as 'Dear Customer' or may, using modern computer technology, be personalised by merging the customer's name and address with the standard letter. Examples are given in the second half of this book.

To produce a standard form letter file, analyse the replies you send out over a period of time and see what similar paragraphs are frequently repeated. Decide on the most satisfactory variant of each of these. These paragraphs can then be put into indexed and classified files. At least two identical copies, one for the writer and one for the typist, will be needed. Alternatively such files could of course be computerised if you have a word processor. Then, when planning and dictating a letter you can simply say 'standard paragraph 2', etc. However, in order to make individual letters seem less impersonal and to help paragraphs flow into one another more smoothly it may be necessary for you or your typist to add suitable linking words or phrases. Like printed letters, your standard form letter file will need periodic updating.

Example 4 A printed or duplicated letter

PRINTED LETTERHEADING

Your ref: ....   (for date) ....

(for recipient's name
and address)
....
....
....

Dear ....

Thank you for your enquiry about our range of
....

We are pleased to enclose an illustrated leaflet which gives
details of the range together with our current price list.

We look forward to receiving an order from you.

Yours sincerely

....
for Company Name

Enc

Dictation

Letters can be dictated either on to a machine for audio typing, or to a
shorthand typist. Both methods have their advantages and disadvantages.

Dictation on to a machine, in particular a portable one, can be done at
any time it suits you and saves the shorthand typist's time. It is usually
possible to play back the recording to check your letter before it is typed,
and there is also no danger of errors due to faulty shorthand. However,
machine dictation is not a good idea if you have a strong accent or a
stammer, and it is also more difficult for the typist to clear up any points
which are not instantly obvious.

If you dictate into a machine you should speak clearly and deliberately,
although most audio typists will be able to cope with a normal speech
speed. Keep a constant distance from the microphone or phone receiver so

that the recording volume remains constant and, if possible, dictate in a quiet location where background phone bells, typewriters, etc, are least likely to interrupt the recording.

If you are dictating to a shorthand typist both you and the typist should start the dictation session well prepared. You will need to have sorted your papers into a logical order, have notes of the main points you wish to cover, and have dealt with any phone calls you can so that they do not interrupt.

For either type of dictation certain basic principles apply, but they are particularly important in audio dictating where it is more difficult to clear up any points omitted or unclear.

You should start the dictation with details of what you are about to dictate. This might include the type of correspondence (particularly if it is something other than a normal letter), the type of headed paper (if more than one type is used), the letter's rough length (so that the typist can use suitably sized paper), the typeface required (if there is more than one available), the number of copies needed (and whether these should be carbon copies or photocopies), and any unusual style features (eg if you want the letter double spaced when the normal style used is single spaced).

Include details of the recipient's name and address, reference codes, etc, and indicate the style of opening greeting required. (You may of course provide these details in an accompanying correspondence file.) Spell out any difficult or unusual words or names and any technical terms, but don't insult your typist's intelligence by constantly repeating the same spelling. You will also need to indicate any words (other than sentence beginnings) which should have an initial capital or be in all capitals or underlined, and don't forget that it makes the typist's job much easier if he or she is told this before, not after, the word! It is not usually necessary to state punctuation as this should be obvious from the way you speak, but it may be useful to indicate new paragraphs. Dub over any changes you make, and don't forget to indicate the end of the letter to prevent any possible confusion.

Both you and your typist will find dictation much easier if you use short clear sentences — if you can't remember the whole sentence at once it's probably too long and convoluted.

Longhand drafts

Although it will take more of your time to produce a longhand draft than to dictate a letter, longhand drafts do have the advantage that you can see the whole of your letter before it is typed and can easily make any necessary revisions. It is often a good idea to read your longhand draft aloud, as this will give you a good idea of how it will sound to your recipient, and your revision should aim at cutting out any superfluous or long-winded statements (while still retaining clarity).

Typists can cope with nearly all handwriting once it is familiar, but if your writing is really appalling you may do best to type out a rough draft yourself — however poor your typing. Otherwise it is best to use lined paper and to use only one side of the paper as this makes it much easier for the typist to follow and also allows you to cut and restick to change the order of parts of your letter if necessary. Try to indicate the layout by the way you write on the page (this is particularly important when you have columns of figures, etc); you may wish to add explanatory notes to the typist, too. These notes should be encircled to indicate that they are clearly not for typing. The correct spellings of names or technical words which the typist may not be able to read easily should be shown in encircled capital letters in the margin. When you revise your letter make any alterations as neatly as possible following the standard correction signs (see Appendix D). Use lines crossed through the whole of the word or phrase to be deleted, and if you have a whole sentence or paragraph to insert it may be best to write it on a separate sheet of paper and indicate the position by a circled A, B, etc. Be particularly careful to make sure insertions are clearly marked. It is most infuriating to a typist to get to the bottom of a page and find an extra sentence with a pale pencil line (previously unseen) leading to its correct position! (However, a good typist should guard against such problems by reading the draft through before starting to type.)

Typing

This section is aimed at the two-finger typist — the individual typing his or her own business letters at home, or the small business which does not as yet run to a professional secretary. Even when typing with two fingers it is easy to follow certain basic typing rules and conventions, and this should lead to a more professional appearance to your letters.

Firstly you should make sure you are really familiar with your typewriter and all it can do. Many typewriters have 'Tab' buttons which will enable you to line up indentations and columns, and the instruction booklet should tell you how to use this facility. Also check the ribbon — an old, dried-up fabric ribbon will spoil even the best typing, and if you want your typing to look very black and clear it may be worth investing in a carbon film ribbon. Finally, when you are not taking carbon copies always get into the habit of using a sheet of spare paper as a backing sheet behind your typing paper as this will help prolong the life of the typewriter's platen as well as improving the appearance of the typing. Also, if you mark a heavy line on the backing paper about 40 mm ($1\frac{1}{2}$ inches) up from the bottom of the paper this will show through the top paper so that you can see when you are approaching the end of the sheet.

Most typewriter typefaces come in two basic sizes: elite (which has 12 characters to an inch) and pica (10 characters to an inch). Typewriter type in both elite and pica faces usually takes up a standard space down the page, and you will probably have room for six lines of single-spaced typing per inch. Armed with this information it is possible to work out how many characters (letters plus spaces) across a page and how many lines down a page will fit on a specific size of paper, and this will help you to judge how much space your letter will take up and thus the best layout. The total numbers of characters and lines which could be fitted on A4 and A5 paper (making no allowance for margins) are given below:

Paper size	Characters across page		Lines down page
	elite	pica	
A4	100	82	70
A5 (portrait)	70	59	50
A5 (landscape)	100	82	35

One of the most common indications of non-professional typing is narrow margins. On A4 paper you should normally leave at least six lines (25 mm/1 inch) at the top and bottom of the page and 10-15 characters pica/12-18 characters elite (25-40mm/1-1$\frac{1}{2}$ inches) for left and right margins. Obviously smaller margins would be acceptable on A5 paper. You will want your letter to look reasonably centred on the page, and if your letter is short you may consider it will look best typed in 1$\frac{1}{2}$ or double spacing. It is normal to leave a line space between all the parts of the letter detailed in the layout section and as shown in the examples, but you may need to vary this to get a good overall layout. However, you should make sure you leave plenty of space for the signature — six lines will take most signatures, but you will need more for particularly flourishing signatures.

Decide on the style of layout you intend to use and stick to it. If you use a blocked style practically everything will be lined up on the left margin, but if you use semi-blocked or indented styles you should set a 'Tab' button for the paragraph indentation (five characters is the normal indentation used), and you will also have to line up any sender's address at the top right, and centre any subject heading and the complimentary close.

The sender's address should be lined up by working out the longest line and counting back from your right-hand margin that number of characters. All of the address is then typed to line up at this point.

Centring of headings (and columns in tables, etc) is done by calculating the number of character spaces available and halving it to give the centre of the typed area. In a similar fashion work out the number of characters needed for the heading (add one if you end up with an odd number) and halve it. Then if you backspace the half number of characters needed for the heading from the central point in the type area you will be at the correct position to start typing your heading. Quicker, still, backspace from the centre of the typed area counting off pairs of letters in the heading.

The complimentary close is in fact not usually exactly centred, and if you use A4 paper aligned with the zero point of the scale bar on the typewriter you will find that the complimentary close looks right if started at about 50 characters across in a pica type or 55 characters in an elite type. All the parts of the close should, of course, line up.

If you need to run on to a continuation sheet you should include details of the recipient's name, the date (both as given on the main letter), and the page number. There are two main styles of doing this which are used with the fully blocked and semi-blocked styles, as illustrated.

Fully blocked

(turn down four lines)
Page number
(one line space)
Date
(one line space)
Recipient's name
(one line space)
(continue main body of letter)

Semi-blocked

(turn down four lines)
Recipient's name   Page number   Date
(one line space)
(continue main body of letter)

You should avoid leaving just the complimentary close on a continuation sheet; if necessary start the new page a couple of lines back in the last paragraph and leave a larger bottom margin on the first sheet.

There are also recognised rules when typing for the amount of space to leave around punctuation. Commas, semi-colons and colons should all be closed up to the character before them, with a single space after them. Fullstops, question marks and exclamation marks are likewise closed up to the character before but are followed by two spaces. Dashes used as punctuation (eg instead of brackets) should have a space either side of them, whereas hyphens should be closed up to the letters on either side.

Abbreviations such as Esq can be used with or without fullstops — the system you use should tie in with whether you are using open or closed punctuation. However, abbreviations for units such as cm, kg, lb, etc, should not be followed by a fullstop (nor should an 's' be added for plurals). Other generally accepted conventions include the use of either a pound or a p sign for quantities of money (ie £5.07, £0.97, 97p) but not both (ie not £5.07p). Words rather than figures should be used for numbers at the beginnings of sentences but otherwise try and adhere to a system (eg words for numbers up to ten and figures above, or figures for all numbers). It is also acceptable to use either commas or spaces in numbers over a thousand (ie 10 000 or 10,000) but choose and stick to one or the other style and relate it to the punctuation style you are using.

If you are typing columns of figures you should line the numbers up on the decimal point, and overall totals should be indicated by double underlining (underline as normal then turn down the cylinder very slightly and underline again). Table headings or columns can be centred (for the semi-blocked style) by applying the same principles as with headings, and at least three spaces should be left between the longest line of each column of a table for clarity.

Unless you have a very sophisticated typewriter there will probably be some characters you cannot easily type. These can be added by hand later, but certain characters can be produced by combining two or more typewriter keys:

exclamation mark   !   (fullstop plus apostrophe)
dollar sign $ (capital S plus solidus)
square brackets   [(solidus with underlining line top and bottom)
equals sign   =   (two hyphens with cylinder turned up slightly between them)
asterisk   x $\pm$ (small x plus hyphen or plus sign)

Unusual fractions should be typed as 3/5, etc, but should not be mixed with $\frac{1}{2}$-type fractions available directly from the typewriter. Superior or inferior characters (eg the degree sign in °C or the 'squared' part of km^2) are produced by turning the cylinder up or down half a line (use a small 'oh' for the degree sign) — but remember to turn back to the correct line afterwards.

By thinking ahead, try and avoid splitting words at the ends of lines, but when you have to break a word try and do so at a sensible place based on the sense and/or the pronunciation of the word. There are dictionaries of standard word-breaks available which can give guidance.

Minor errors, neatly corrected, are probably acceptable in most business correspondence (as long as you are not applying for a typist's job!) but if the letter gets really messy a retype would be worthwhile. Otherwise there are several correction methods available. If you use a typing rubber you should move the carriage along to one extreme or the other to prevent bits of rubber falling into the machine and clogging up the works. You will also need to protect any carbon copies by inserting pieces of paper between the sheets, and you will have to make corrections on the carbons separately. Correction papers are useful for correcting the odd incorrect letter and work on the principle of typing over the incorrect letter in white and then typing the correct letter on top. However, the correction can rub off under pressure. Typing correction fluids are probably better for more major changes but need to be used carefully to avoid large coloured lumps. They must be allowed to dry fully to prevent both messy corrections and the clogging up of your typewriter keys. Both correction papers and fluids can be obtained in certain colours and may be useful if you are not using white paper.

Self-correcting ribbons used together with carbon film are used in a similar way to correction papers — the incorrect letter is overtyped (but is actually lifted off by the correction ribbon) then the correct letter is substituted. However, this facility is only available on certain typewriters.

Although you should obviously try to layout your letter in a standard way there are techniques which can be used to 'rescue' letters rather than retyping them. As mentioned in the notes on the fully blocked style the date is sometimes placed on the right of the letter, opposite the reference code, and this position could be used if you miss out the date and don't have room to add it at the left margin. The recipient's name and address is sometimes typed at the bottom left of the letter, so this position could be used if you've missed it above, and the 'for the attention of' line could, of course, be used instead of the recipient's name line if this has been omitted.

Finally, always get into the habit of checking your typing before you take it out of the machine as any corrections can be made more neatly at this stage.

Checking

As well as checking obvious points like spellings of names against past correspondence, the typist should also check anything else easily dealt with — for example if a letter refers to a meeting on Wednesday 4 July check that 4 July really is a Wednesday! He or she should also check the letter when completed for typing errors and spelling or punctuation mistakes before returning it for signing.

However, the typist may have read your writing wrongly or may have made a mistake in transcribing the shorthand, so the writer should also check the letter before it is signed and posted. You may find some mistakes that the typist has overlooked or some errors in what you said or wrote in the first place. Any corrections needed should be either marked on the top copy lightly with a soft pencil or can be made more obviously on a carbon copy or photocopy. As with correcting longhand drafts use standard corrections signs (see Appendix D) as far as possible (though on the top copy you will want to make the minimum number of marks), and circle round any notes to the typist. If corrections are few these can probably be made neatly on the top copy (a thin drawing pen is often useful for these), but if there are many corrections it may be almost as quick and certainly neater to get the letter retyped.

Finally, before sealing the envelope check that all enclosures mentioned have been included.

Copying

You should keep a copy of all business letters for your files. Copies have traditionally been made by taking carbon copies, but today many businesses take photocopies. These have the advantage of showing the letter as finally sent: carbon copies *should* be corrected and amended to match the top copy but this does not always happen. Some businesses make a carbon copy on the back of the letter being answered: this has the advantage of keeping both parts of the correspondence together. You may also need extra copies to send for information to other people, and with most typewriters it is possible to get up to six or so readable copies. Using special thin paper and/or double-sided carbon paper (which prints an image on the back of a sheet which is transparent enough to be read from the front) it is sometimes possible to get up to about 12 copies. Special carbons are made for typing rather than writing; you should also check carbons periodically and throw out any that have come to the end of their useful life. You can also buy NCR (no carbon required) paper. This special paper contains a chemical which produces a coloured substance under pressure from the typewriter keys, and produces a neat-looking copy as well as being easy to handle.

There are a variety of different photocopying processes. Some of the cheaper desk-top copiers are slow and need special papers (often giving copies with a shiny surface). Such copiers can be useful to small businesses for making file copies, but the quality may not be good enough to use for letters to be sent out. Larger electrostatic photocopiers are much more expensive but most can use any type of paper (including headed notepaper) and they may offer other facilities such as double-sided copying, enlargement or reduction, etc.

While photocopiers are convenient for producing smallest numbers of copies, for large numbers of copies of circular letters, etc, one of the following methods of duplication may be more appropriate.

1 Stencilling: the letter is typed on a stencil skin which is then transferred to a duplicating machine. The method and equipment are relatively cheap, simple drawings, signatures, etc, can be added by using a special stylus pen, and up to about 5000 copies can be produced from a stencil. It is also possible to make stencils photographically from a master copy typed on normal paper. Stencils can be stored for future use, and it is also possible to introduce colour by using a separate stencil and duplication run for each colour.

2 Spirit duplicating: this process, which is very rarely used for business letters nowadays, depends on special coated papers which are used like carbon papers to produce master sheets. It is possible, by overtyping with different coloured papers, to introduce several colours on to the master. However, images tend to be fuzzy and it is only possible to get 250 or so copies from a master.

3 Offset litho: a special copier is used to prepare the plates for offset litho and these plates can be made of paper, plastic or metal depending on the number of copies required. It is possible to duplicate up to 50 000 or so copies from a single plate. The copies can be printed on most types of paper and are of a better quality than those produced by stencilling or spirit duplicating. The equipment needed for offset litho is not cheap and needs a skilled operator, but once you have the equipment the copies themselves are fairly cheap. Machines for offset litho and photocopying will probably be outside the price range of many small businesses, but there are, of course, many business service and copying centres where such work is undertaken.

Word processors

Until about 1979 typewriters were neatly all either mechanical or electric (electromechanical). Golfball typeheads and self-correcting mechanisms helped to improve the quality of type and speed attainable and made it easy to change print style, and electromechanical machines were much quieter and generally easier to use. Since 1979 there have been rapid developments in electronic typewriters and word processors (with microchips rather than moving parts). Although the 'old faithful' will probably be quite adequate for many individuals and small businesses, a very brief summary of some of the functions available with word processing equipment is given below to help you decide whether such a machine would help you with your business letter writing. There is now a large variety of machines available at widely ranging prices (and discounts), and also plenty of salesmen only too keen to sell you their brand of equipment, so you would be well advised to read all the business equipment magazines and books you can lay your hands on, as well as talking to people who already have word processors, before deciding what, if anything, to buy.

The first level up from a mechanical or electric typewriter is an electronic machine. These usually have daisy wheel typeheads, and have facilities to help you correct and edit small blocks of text. They often include features such as automatic centring, variable type sizes, etc. They may also have memories, and a small display panel which enables you to see and correct a few words of text before committing them to paper. However, the memory usually only operates while the machine is switched on, which may impose limitations. (Some machines will retain the information in the memories if left plugged in but 'off'.) However, they do have more facilities than most electromechanical models and are now largely superseding them for much office use.

There is a degree of overlap between electronic typewriters and screenless word processors — the next level up. Screenless word processors have some form of storage facility (usually disks) which enable you to store material from one work session to another even when the machine is switched off. They can perform many of the normal word processing functions but, as the name indicates, they do not have a screen to show the text — it is committed directly to paper. They also tend to be slower in operation than word processors with screens.

A machine which is specifically designed for word processing is known as a dedicated word processor. It is also possible to obtain word processing software for microcomputers (which can also, of course, perform other functions such as accounting if other programs are used) but again the boundaries are blurred: some 'dedicated' word processors offer other office-type functions such as bookkeeping programs, for instance. The word processing programs in both dedicated word processors and microcomputers are also usually stored on disks (which enables them to be replaced by an updated or modified program) and the machine will have disk (or occasionally cassette tape) storage for the text entered. The material entered or stored on disks is displayed on a screen and can be edited in this form before being 'printed out'. Most machines allow concurrent printing — text can be printed out while you work on other text. The standard of print-out depends on the printer used — some use a dot matrix (each character is made up of a series of dots) which may make the characters to appear not quite solid, but the more expensive printers produce a much higher quality type.

What are the processes you can undertake with a word processor, or a computer word processing program? Obviously the different machines have varying functions, which is why you need to work out carefully what is important to you. However, the main types of functions available are:

1 Editing functions: making corrections, including a certain change to the same word throughout a block of text (eg a 'Mr Browne' wrongly spelt 'Brown' throughout a letter could be corrected in one go). Deleting, inserting, or replacing letters, words, sentences and even whole paragraphs throughout the text. Moving blocks of text. Searching for certain words or symbols throughout the text.
2 Display functions: centring, justification, variable line lengths, type sizes and styles. Once the parameters are set a certain layout can be followed just by calling up details from the memory.
3 Merging of disks: for example standard letter can be merged with a name and address list to produce a 'personalised' circular letter.

Programs are also available to carry out such tasks as checking spellings against a word list stored on disk, sorting items into alphabetical order and making straightforward calculations.

It takes time and training to make full use of a word processor's possibilities, and it really depends on the kind of business letters you send as to whether a word processor would be helpful. You may, of course have other uses for a word processor or microcomputer which may affect your decisions. The more repetitive the letters, the more benefits there are from a word processor — the word processor can store the contents of your standard letter form file and be used in the same way. The facilities for merging disks can be useful for circular letters, and word processors have obvious benefits for reworking drafts of letters — as the whole letter is not retyped each time there is less chance of new errors being introduced. Word processors are also useful for storing address lists (which can easily be updated) for labels, etc. However, a small office producing straight-forward but variable letters would probably have trouble justifying the initial expenses against the likely benefits.

Other office machines

There are machines available to open letters, others to collate, fold or insert letters and seal envelopes, and you can also buy electronic letter scales which can be programmed with the current postage rates.

Other machines are available for letter addressing. One of these may be useful if you regularly send out large numbers of circular letters to the same people. The various types of addressing machines available are similar in function to the duplicating machines described previously — the addresses are typed once on to a stencil, offset litho or spirit type master copy and can then be run off on to the envelopes or labels.

Another machine worth considering if you have large amounts of mail to send out is a franking machine. Franking gives advantages in that you do not have to go out and buy individual stamps, and you can also include a business logo, address or advertisement in the frank, but you do have to pay the post office in advance, and it may be difficult to correct mistakes if the wrong postage is entered and stamped on a letter.

Filing

The primary purpose of filing business letters is to provide a readily available record of past correspondence. Files should also include notes from phone calls, etc, to provide a complete record of information on a particular subject or correspondent.

There are many different systems available, but certain basic principles apply however you file your letters. Firstly, files must be kept up to date and tidy. It's no good knowing you have been in touch with a certain person if you can't find past correspondence because it is in the large pile labelled 'for filing' and not yet readily accessible in its own file. The latest correspondence should be kept to the top or in front (as it is most likely to be needed for reference) and you will also need periodically to remove non-current material from files and transfer it to longer-term storage files so that current matter doesn't get swamped by old correspondence. Avoid paper clips in filing systems: they can easily catch on other papers. Either staple papers together or leave them as individual sheets.

Whatever system you choose for filing should ideally retain flexibility for expansion or adaption to cope with your changing needs. The simplest systems are box files, ring binders or cardboard envelope files, and these are probably adequate for most individuals storing business letters. A 'personal file' with letter or number codes will give you more flexibility than one of the files sold ready-labelled 'bank', 'mortgage', 'insurance', etc; everyone's exact filing needs differ.

Small businesses will probably need some kind of filing cabinet. These can be of the traditional type (with drawers) or a 'lateral' file which has the advantage of using less office space for the same number of files. The cabinets usually come with pockets which are labelled, and the letters themselves are put into a cardboard folder which is stored in the appropriate pocket. When a file is required the folder as a whole is taken out rather than individual letters, and this means that there is less chance of losing individual letters or of replacing files in the wrong order.

Files can be placed in alphabetical, numerical, alphanumerical, geographical or subject order, all of which have certain advantages and disadvantages.

Alphabetical filing, usually by surnames or key words, is probably the most commonly used system, and is straightforward to follow. It doesn't really matter how you treat names such as McLaren, MacDonald, St John, hyphenated names, etc, as long as you decide on one system and stick to it.

Numerical and alphanumerical systems have the advantages that numbered files are easier to find (and replace correctly) and the system can be expanded more easily than in an alphabetical system, but you will need an index to the numbers to lead you to the correct files. Geographically filed correspondence may be appropriate for certain business (for example those with representatives with geographical territories), and subject filing may be best where the subject matter is more important than the individual names (for example an architect may keep files for all correspondence relating to each project on which he is working).

All filing systems should have 'miscellaneous' files to deal with odd letters not yet justifying a file of their own, and you should also try to develop a cross-referencing system for letters which could be filed (and looked for) in several places. This could consist either of making an extra copy or of using a cross-reference sheet which would include the name, date and a brief résumé of a letter plus the title of the file where the main copy is stored.

Card indexes will probably also be useful if you undertake much business correspondence. These may include just names and addresses, or more sophisticated systems can be developed to provide other details of customers, etc, for use in producing mailing lists.

EMPLOYMENT

Job applications

When writing to a prospective employer, it is important to remember that the letter will be your ambassador. It will create an impression of you in the mind of the recipient on the basis of which he or she will decide whether or not to pursue your application. Obviously you must write or type your letter neatly, laying it out according to the conventions described in the first part of the book. You should include all the *relevant* information, but avoid unnecessary details; remember that the person you are writing to is probably busy. Do not be afraid to let a little of your character show through in your letter, but try not to become chatty.

If you are applying for a post which may involve typing, the letter should be typed as a perfect example of your skill. In other cases a neatly written letter will create a better impression than a badly typed one, but a well typed letter would be better still.

Letter requesting further details and a job application form

15 Oakfield Drive
CARTOWN
Hants
LI12 7RT

29 June 19 -

The Secretary
The Empire Trading Company
Ships Wharf
BRIARLEY
Hants
S05 7RX

Dear Sir

In reply to your advertisement for an Export Manager in *The Echo* (28 June 19-), I would be grateful if you would send me an application form and further details of the post.

Yours faithfully

Frank Binns

Application for a job (no curriculum vitae enclosed)

55 Davidson Avenue
MANCHTER
FP7 7TS

14 September 19 -

Mr H Ody
The Apsley Motor Company
Jowett Road
MANCHTER
MN3 1AK

Dear Mr Ody

I wish to apply for the position of skilled motor mechanic advertised in today's *Manchter Gazette*.

Having completed a full apprenticeship, I have been employed by Jones Motors in the London Road for the past two years. I am now anxious to move to a firm where there are greater prospects for promotion and more interesting work.

My present manager, Mr Brian, has agreed to give me a reference, and I would be free to come for an interview any evening after 4.30 pm.

Yours sincerely

John Collins

If you are already in a job, it is a good idea to explain why you want a change of post, in case anyone might think you are leaving at your employer's behest.

Application for a post—covering letter to accompany curriculum vitae

Hollydene
Collingwood Road
NANTON
Beds
SL5 6XC

10 August 19 -

Box 3998
The Daily Mercury
156 Hope Lane
LONDON
EC3 7YP

Dear Sirs

I am writing in answer to your advertisement in today's *Daily Mercury* for a Sales Representative.

I have had seven years' experience of the type of selling you outline, starting as a trainee with ILC Ltd, and progressing to my present position of Area Sales Representative (South-east) with Jones Brothers of Dunstable. I am now keen to advance my career in a larger organisation with opportunities to engage in overseas selling techniques.

I enclose my curriculum vitae, including the names of two referees. If you think I may be suitable for this position, I should be happy to come for an interview at any time convenient to you.

Yours faithfully

Colin Brown

Enc

There is no need to go into detail about your work experience and qualifications providing your cv covers these adequately.

Curricula vitae in general

The object of a curriculum vitae (sometimes abbreviated to cv) is to set out the details of your education, employment and personal status as a quick reference for the person who requested it. You should always include your name, address and date of birth, and it is normal to give the names and addresses of two referees (ie persons the recipient can refer to regarding your status). Your cv is not the place to write a descriptive essay; just state the facts. It should be written on a separate sheet of paper, enclosed with an explanatory letter, and should be laid out as clearly as possible.

Curriculum vitae

Name: John Smith
Address: 69 Lower Terrace
          Onsworth
          Bedfordshire
          DF7 2SJ
Telephone: home — Onsworth 638006
            office — Onsworth 534662
Date of birth: 8 August 1948
Marital status: married
Education since 11: Penworthy Grammar School
                     Penworthy
                     Bedfordshire
                     FT2 6PN
                     1959 - 66
                     6 'O' levels
                     3 'A' levels History Grade B
                                   Geography Grade C
                                   Latin Grade C
                     Manchter University
                     1966 - 69
                     BA (History) Second Class Hons.
Employment: Management Trainee with Unitech Limited,
             Unitech House, Queen St, Onsworth DB6 6TZ,
             1970 - 71;
             promoted to Assistant Manager (sales) 1971 - 75;

             Area Manager (marketing) with Framley (UK) Ltd,
             Hope House, Thorpe Way, Onsworth DJ2 2PT,
             1975 - present.

Referees: Mr K Park
Sales Manager
Unitech Limited
Unitech House
Queen St
Onsworth
DB6 6TZ

Mr B Crane
Managing Director
Framley (UK) Ltd
Hope House
Thorpe Way
Onsworth
DJ2 2PT

As with any other job application, an enquiry written 'on spec' (see over) must create a good impression on its reader. You will naturally speak of your own abilities, qualifications and experience, but it is also important to say why you think these would be useful to your reader's organisation.

If you would be willing and able to do various jobs, make this clear; but never try to impress by claiming to be able to do things which you cannot in fact manage. State what jobs you really think you can handle, and at what level.

It is a good plan to find out something about the organisation to which you are writing, and then to use what you have discovered in your letter in order to show that you have taken some trouble. If possible, find out the name of the personnel officer or staff manager, and write to him or her in person.

Application 'on spec'

18 Field Gardens
BRIMTON
Beds
AB6 5PR

7 February 19 -

Mr M Davies
Staff Manager
J Bloggs & Sons Ltd
5 Queen's Crescent
BRIMTON
Beds
MB4 PQ8

Dear Mr Davies

I am writing to enquire whether you have any vacancies for a junior office assistant.

I left King Edward's School last Christmas, having passed CSE Examinations in English Language, Geography and French. In my last year at school I also took a course in typing and general office procedures, and I am keen to make proper use of these skills.

Since leaving school I have not been able to find a regular job, but I have done some temporary work with Messrs Smith and Jones, who have been pleased with my work. Mr Smith has himself assured me that he will be quite willing to give me a favourable reference.

I realise that you may not have any vacancies at present, but I would be very willing to work in any department and to undertake any training required. I therefore hope that you will consider my application favourably whenever a possible position arises.

Yours sincerely

Caroline Brown (Miss)

Letter acknowledging a job application

Borset Coast Path Project
St Georges House
St Georges Street
Borchester
B03 6AA

(Date)

(Recipient's name and address)

Dear

Thank you for your application for the post of Information Officer on the Borset Coast Path Project. We have had many applications for this post so I am afraid it will take us some time to sort through them all. However, I would hope that we will be in contact with you again in two or three weeks.

Yours faithfully

Richard Gittins
Project Director

Acknowledgements of job applications are often prepared as circular letters, as in this case.

Letter requesting applicant to attend an interview

Messrs Jones, Smith,
 Brown & Brown
Commercial Chambers
12 King's Road
FARLEIGH
Hants
1SB 4DD

20 October 19 -

Mr M Cox
15 Lindhurst Gardens
OLD POLESFORD
Hants
SL6 8RY

Dear Mr Cox

My partners and I were most interested in your application for the position of Litigation Solicitor at these offices.

We would like to meet you to discuss the position further, and I would therefore be glad if you would telephone my secretary to arrange an appointment as soon as possible.

Yours sincerely
Messrs Jones, Smith, Brown & Brown

Michael Jones

Letter in reply to a request for an interview

25 Oakley Avenue
MILTON
Northants
WR6 9SZ

16 May 19 -

J George Esq
Kingley Marketing
64 King Street
MILTON
Northants
SY7 8PL

Dear Mr George

Thank you very much for your letter of 13 May. I would be happy to come for an interview on 21 May at 2.00 pm, and will bring with me the two references you request.

Yours sincerely

Brian Butts

It is important to send a letter in this situation not merely as a confirmation that you will attend, but also to show that you are taking the matter seriously and pay attention to detail.

Letter to a past employer asking for a reference (from applicant)

25 Oakley Avenue
MILTON
Northants
SY12 4LT

14 May 19 -

Mr B Brown
M & B Creative Marketing
Dower House
PORTON
Northants
RT6 3ER

Dear Mr Brown

I am applying for the post of Salesman with Kingley Marketing of Milton, and I wondered whether you would be willing for me to give your name as a referee.

I have been very happy in my present post, as I was during my four years with M & B, but I have decided to apply for the post with Kingley Marketing as it seems to offer greater responsibility and a chance to use my own initiative more frequently.

Please pass on my regards to any of my colleagues still with M & B and, of course, to Mrs Brown.

Yours sincerely

Brian Butts

Letter following up a reference (from a potential employer)

Kingley Marketing
64 King Street
MILTON
Northants
SY7 8PL

23 May 19 -

B Brown Esq
M & B Creative Marketing
Dower House
PORTON
Northants
RT6 3ER

Dear Mr Brown

Mr Brian Butts, of 25 Oakley Avenue, Milton, has applied to me for the post of Salesman. I understand that he was employed by you for four years in a similar capacity. He has put your name forward as a referee, and I would be most grateful if you would let me know whether you found him capable and totally reliable. I am particularly concerned to know whether, in your experience, he is able to work independently on his own initiative. It goes without saying that whatever you tell me will be treated in the strictest confidence.

I am enclosing a stamped addressed envelope for your reply.

Yours sincerely
Kingley Marketing

John George

Letter of reference

Timber Products Limited
High Lane Estate
MILBORNE
Dorset
YT7 91J

Your ref PR7/8/82
Our ref MD/JL

30 August 19 -

CONFIDENTIAL

The Personnel Manager
Royal Oak Timber Company
MARKYATE
Dorset
RT6 90K

Dear Sir

In reply to your request for information about James Long, who has applied for the position of Works Manager with your company, I can confirm he has been an employee at this company for eight years.

He served a two year apprenticeship with us, and a year later was promoted to Line Foreman. He has always shown himself to be a hard worker and is a popular member of our workforce. Last year we put his managerial skills to the test with promotion to Assistant Works Manager, and we found our decision to be fully justified.

Mr Long is an honest and reliable person and has, I believe, the initiative, experience and capabilities to handle the job for which he has applied.

If you require any further information please do not hesitate to get in touch with me.

Yours faithfully
Royal Oak Timber Company

Michael Deacon
Managing Director

It is always best to send letters of reference to a named individual, and to mark the letter and envelope 'CONFIDENTIAL'.

If you are asked to provide a reference by someone whom you feel you cannot recommend, it is best to refuse politely at the outset. However, if you *have* to write a reference for such a person, you should state the fact that you have reservations, while trying to avoid any specific accusations.

Writing a favourable reference is much easier, but remember to keep your recommendation relevant to the nature of the job applied for.

Letter offering employment

Messrs Jones, Smith,
   Brown & Brown
12 King's Road
FARLEIGH
Hants
ISB 4DD

4 November 19 -

Mr M Cox
15 Lindhurst Gardens
OLD POLESFORD
Hants
SL6 8RY

Dear Mr Cox

I am delighted to tell you that my partners and I have decided to offer you the post of Litigation Solicitor with our firm.

Since you told me that you must give one month's notice to your present employers, it would seem sensible for you not to take up your position here until 2 January next. I have entered this date on the enclosed contract of employment, which I would ask you to sign and return to me as soon as possible.

I hope you will enjoy working at Jones Smith Brown & Brown.

Yours sincerely
Jones, Smith, Brown & Brown

Michael Jones

Enc

Letter accepting an offer of employment

9 Poole Road
OXRIDGE
Bucks
SL9 6TB

15 October 19-

R Burns Esq
Personnel Manager
Timetec Limited
Rose Estate
OXRIDGE
Bucks
SL9 5RF

Dear Mr Burns

Thank you for your letter of 12 October offering me the post of Ledger Clerk with your organisation.

I am delighted to accept the position and look forward to starting work with you on 15 November.

Yours sincerely

Jane Allcock (Miss)

Letter rejecting an offer of employment

9 Poole Road
OXRIDGE
Bucks
SL9 6TB

15 October 19-

R Burns Esq
Personnel Manager
Timetec Limited
Rose Estate
OXRIDGE
Bucks
SL9 5RF

Dear Mr Burns

Thank you very much for your letter of 12 October offering me
the post of Ledger Clerk with your organisation.

I am afraid that after much careful thought I have decided that I
cannot accept the position. As I explained when we met, I am
really looking for a job with greater possibilities for broadening
my experience in the accountancy field, and I have now been
offered just such a post.

I hope that my decision will not inconvenience you, and I would
like to thank you for your confidence in my abilities.

Yours sincerely

Jane Allcock (Miss)

Letter rejecting a job application

Timetec Limited
Rose Estate
OXRIDGE
Bucks
SL9 5RF

13 October 19-

Miss Jane Allcock
9 Poole Road
OXRIDGE
Bucks
SL9 6TB

Dear Miss Allcock

I am afraid that after careful consideration I have decided that I cannot offer you the position of Ledger Clerk.

You undoubtedly have considerable ability but, as I explained at your interview, we are looking for someone with rather more experience.

Thank you very much for your time in attending for interview.

Yours sincerely
Timetec Limited

Roger Burns

Letters involving a refusal or rejection are often awkward to write. It is important to be firm, but never rude or harsh, and while it is often helpful to give your reasons, white lies are normally best avoided.

At Work

Letter enquiring about promotion prospects

2 Hornsby Terrace
UPTON
Surrey
SU8 3WE

5 June 19-

Ms K Tope
Accounts Manager
Smith & Co. Ltd
54-58 Pine Road
UPTON
Surrey
SU4 5RF

Dear Ms Tope

I am writing to ask whether you would consider promoting me to the position of Senior Clerk.

As you know, I have been working for the Company for four years, one year as Junior Clerk and three years as Clerk.

I have undertaken the work of Senior Clerk during periods of holiday and sickness and, apart from finding the work very interesting, I believe that I have performed it satisfactorily.

I have a number of ideas for improving the efficiency of the Department which the scope of my present job does not allow me to implement.

I would be grateful for the opportunity to discuss this matter.

Yours sincerely

Robert Smith

Letter asking for transfer to a different department

Laboratory B5

3 April 19-

Mr H Green
Personnel Manager
Block H

Dear Mr Green

I am writing to request a transfer to laboratory B1. There are two principal reasons for this request.

Firstly, I am particularly interested in some of the problems which this laboratory plans to initiate research on. Secondly, a personality clash has arisen over the past few months, which I find very disturbing. I have, otherwise, been very happy during my three years of employment here.

I feel that my knowledge and experience would be equally well suited to the work in laboratory B1. The project I have been working on for the past year should be comleted in a month and it would create the minimum disturbance if I transferred then.

I hope that you will give this matter your favourable consideration.

Yours sincerely

Jane White

Letter asking for unpaid leave (compassionate)

4 Farren Road
LONDON
SE6 8UH

2 July 19-

Mr Nichols
Sales Manager
Grant & Sons Ltd
19 Church Lane
LONDON
SE4 91G

Dear Mr Nichols

I would be grateful to receive your permission for me to be absent from work next week (8-12 July).

I am needed to look after my mother, who is an invalid, during this week. The person who normally looks after her is required urgently elsewhere next week. At such short notice, I have been unable to arrange alternative care. This is an exceptional situation, which I do not anticipate recurring.

I hope that you will give my request sympathetic consideration. I appreciate that I would not be paid for this week.

Yours sincerely

Jane Ryman

If granted paid compassionate leave, omit the last sentence.

Letter excusing absence from work because of own illness

15 Greenland Road
SAMPTER
Essex
ES3 8UJ

3 December 19-

Mr H Jones
Head of Sales Department
Hampton & Co Ltd
12-14 High Street
SAMPTER
Essex
ES7 4ED

Dear Mr Jones

I left a telephone message with your secretary this morning to explain that I was feeling unwell, and was going to visit my doctor. He has diagnosed an infection of the respiratory tract, and suggested I would probably need to be off work for at least ten days. I enclose a medical certificate.

I have spoken to John Griffiths about my work commitments for the next few days and I believe that things are under control, but if anybody has any problems about my work they should not hesitate to telephone me.

Yours sincerely

Gerald Long

Enc

Letter excusing absence from work because of a relative's death

2 Creek Avenue
FORSHAM
Lancs
LA5 9CV

23 September 19-

Dear Mr Smith

I regret that I was not at work today and will be unable to attend for the rest of the week. My father died suddenly yesterday evening and I am needed here to help settle his affairs and to make arrangements for the funeral. Also, the whole family, including myself, are very shaken by his death.

I expect to be back at work on Monday 29 September.

Yours sincerely

Carol Brown

In letters like this — which verge on the personal — the recipient's address can be omitted.

Letter from employer in reply to notification of death of a relative of employee

Crane Co Ltd
48 Bridge
Lane
CROXFORD
Lancs
LA5 4PD

25 September 19-

Ms C Brown
2 Creek Avenue
FORSHAM
Lancs
LA5 9CV

Dear Carol

I was very sorry to learn of your father's death. It must have been a terrible shock for you. I sympathize with you and all your family on your bereavement.

I look forward to seeing you again on 29 September, if you are able to conclude your father's affairs by then.

Yours sincerely

Craig Smith

This type can be among the most difficult of letters to write, for obvious reasons. There is no need to dwell on the illness or death which may be the subject of your letter, although your letter should, of course, convey the sympathy which is intended. Letters should normally be brief and to the point.

Letter of complaint about facilities at work place

Accounts Department
Third floor

6 February 19-

Ms D Kenny
Personnel Manager
Fifth floor

Dear Ms Kenny

I wish to draw your attention to the washing facilities on the third floor. Only one sink is provided for over one hundred male employees on this floor. There is usually neither soap nor clean towels available.

This must be detrimental to the health of employees and is certainly a waste of the Company's money since much work time is lost in queuing for the use of these inadequate facilities.

I would be grateful if you would look into this matter urgently, with a view to providing adequate, well-maintained facilities.

Yours sincerely

On behalf of the Accounts Department
John Harris

Letter offering resignation

4 Oak Road
Creigh
ALSOP
Yorks
NO7 3SD

29 September 19 -

Mr D Hobbis
Sales Manager
Creen & Sons Ltd
25 Weldon Road
LEEDS
LE1 8NM

Dear Mr Hobbis

I have been offered, and have decided to accept, the position of Sales Manager with Broom & Sons Ltd. I am writing, therefore, to give you the appropriate four weeks' notice to terminate my employment with the Company on 27 October.

I have been very happy during my five years here and it was with some sorrow that I reached this decision. However, my new position offers considerably more scope and responsibility than my present one.

I would like to take this opportunity to thank you for all the support and guidance you have given me over the past five years.

Yours sincerely

Frank Rane

If you have not been happy in your employment, you may want to omit the last two paragraphs.

Letter accepting resignation

Creen & Sons Ltd
25 Weldon Road
LEEDS
LE1 8NM

1 October 19 -

Mr Frank Rane
4 Oak Road
Creigh
ALSOP
Yorks
NO7 3SD

Dear Frank

Thank you for your letter of 29 September resigning your employment with the Company on 27 October, which I accept with reluctance.

Your new position seems to be an excellent opportunity, which you richly deserve. I am only sorry that the Company cannot offer you anything comparable at the present time.

I am grateful for the initiative and enthusiasm which you have brought to your job over the past five years and wish you every success in the future.

Yours sincerely

David Hobbis

Letter of warning from an employer (unofficial)

Sales and Marketing Limited
Langdon House
Ship Street
READING
Berkshire
DT6 8UH

16 August 19 -

Mr Brian Coulsden
12 Tree Drive
Oakley
READING
Berks
LY9 7UN

Dear Mr Coulsden,

I am afraid that I must write to you concerning your persistent late arrival at this office. It has not gone unnoticed, and if it continues I shall be forced to take the matter to higher authority.

If you have any problem which has a bearing on this matter, please do not hesitate to come and talk to me about it. I am sure we would both prefer a solution that did not involve disciplinary action.

Yours sincerely
Sales and Marketing Limited

Peter Garton
Personnel Manager

Letter of reply to a warning letter

12 Tree Drive
Oakley
READING
Berks
LY9 7UN

18 August 19 -

Mr Peter Garton
Personnel Manager
Sales and Marketing Limited
Langdon House
Ship Street
READING
Berks
DT6 8UH

Dear Mr Garton

In reply to your letter of 16 August, first of all may I apologise for causing you to have to write to me on such a matter.

My wife is in hospital at present, recovering from a major operation, and I have therefore had to get our two children ready for school before leaving for work. I have now spoken to a neighbour who has most kindly agreed to come in on three mornings a week to help us. Unfortunately she is not available on Thursdays or Fridays, and I would be grateful for your understanding on these days. I will continue to make up the time during the lunch interval, but I am afraid that in the circumstances it is hard for me to stay late in the evenings.

I realise now that I should have explained the situation to you earlier, and hope that you will accept my apologies.

Yours sincerely

Brian Coulsden

Letter to an employee giving notice of termination of employment

Universal Products Ltd
Crown House
Marshall Street
SOUTHWICK
Surrey
NF3 6JP

28 March 19 -

Mr D Bull
1 Bracken Close
SOUTHWICK
Surrey
NF6 7EW

Dear Mr Bull

I very much regret having to write this letter. However, despite numerous verbal and two written warnings you have continued to arrive late at work. In addition, you have been insolent to your departmental manager Mr Davies on a number of occasions when he has reminded you about your timekeeping.

The company feels that you have been given sufficient time to mend your ways or to sort out any problems you may have had relating to this, and I am afraid I now have no alternative but to give you four weeks' notice of termination of employment with Universal Products Ltd.

Yours sincerely

N Chatterton
Personnel Manager

This letter would be preceded by a similarly worded letter stating that it was a 'final warning' so that the employee could not claim that he had received inadequate warning about his conduct.

TRADING

Letter to a supplier requesting details of goods/services

25 Samson Lane
SALHOUSE
Yorks
SL8 5RF

1 October 19 -

Champion Gates Limited
Furlong Road
SALHOUSE
Yorks
RT7 6YN

Dear Sir

I have seen your advertisement in *Gardening Weekly*, and I would be grateful for some further details about your wrought iron gates, as follows:

1 Can you supply double gates to fit an opening 2.3 metres wide?
2 What type of gate posts do you recommend?
3 Can the gates be delivered, and if so at what charge?
4 Could you send me a brochure showing the styles you have available?

I look forward to your reply.

Yours faithfully

Thomas Crane

If you have several questions within a letter it may be useful to number points so that the person replying can easily check that they have dealt with all your queries.

Such an enquiry would not normally be accompanied by a stamped addressed envelope as the supplier hopes to do trade with you and therefore will expect to pay postage. However, read advertisements carefully; sometimes you will be asked to send an SAE for a catalogue or similar.

Letter from a retailer to a supplier requesting details about goods

Greenfingers Garden Supplies Ltd
Mill Lane
DROSFORD
Wilts
DO4 7NB

5 June 19 -

Umow Lawnmowers Ltd
54-58 Fern Road
TIPLON
West Midlands
B16 7AJ

Dear Sirs

Please send us a catalogue of your full lawnmower range, and supply us with details regarding trade terms.

At the same time perhaps you could tell us how soon we might expect delivery after placing an order, and what the position is regarding after-sales service.

Yours faithfully
Greenfingers Garden Supplies Ltd

Richard Miles

A retailer writing to a supplier will generally need several different sorts of information: eg the products available; the terms of sale (costs, discounts, whether on a sale or return arrangement, the period allowed for paying, etc), and delivery times.

Letter from a supplier replying to retailer giving details of goods/services

Umow Lawnmowers Ltd
54-58 Fern Road
TIPLON
West Midlands
B16 7AJ

10 June 19 -

Mr Richard Miles
Greenfingers Garden Supplies Ltd
Mill Lane
DROSFORD
Wilts
DO4 7NB

Dear Mr Miles

Thank you for your letter of 5 June.

We have pleasure in enclosing our catalogue of lawnmowers.

Our terms are 30 days nett from date of invoice.

We normally hope to make deliveries within three to four weeks of receipt of order. However, I am afraid that delivery of Model TE7 may currently take up to six weeks, due to production difficulties. We hope, however, to resolve these problems within the next couple of months.

Spares for all current models are readily available from us, and we also operate a regular free collect and delivery repair service for our dealers.

Our Southern Representative, Mr John Spears of 15 Rose Way, Gromsey, Hants (telephone Gromsey 45219) would, of course, be pleased to call on you at your request.

Yours sincerely

Harry Treen
Sales Department

Letter requesting goods advertised in a publication

8 Birchfield Drive
ACTONBURY ABBAS
Dorset
DN4 3DD

16 September 19 -

Countryways Fashion Wear Ltd
Countryways House
North Temple Street
LEEDS
LN6 1RR

Dear Sirs

Please send me one pair of 'Elegant Rider' fashion boots as advertised in issue 24 of *Countryside* magazine at £39.50. I require a pair of size 5 boots, preferably in dark tan. My second choice colour is old English green.

I enclose a cheque in the sum of £42.00 to include postage and packing.

Yours faithfully

Caroline Lockwood

Letter placing an order

Goodbooks
18 Middens Way
EAST RENICK
Strathclyde
RE5 8JT

4 May 19 -

Henry & Jones (Publishers) Ltd
42 Parade Street
EDINBURGH
ED1 6DH

Dear Sirs

Please supply the following books as listed in your January to July 19 - catalogue.

Quantity	Title	Author	ISBN
3	Metaphysical Plurality	Junkett	28975 8
5	Scientific Communication	Duncan and Yole	34661 9
10	Music in the 19th Century	Nicol	27765 0

I understand that you will supply these books on a sale or return basis at a discount of 25% but that I will be liable for carriage.

Yours faithfully

Helen Baird (Mrs)

Many firms will have their own standardised order forms, but if you order by letter you should make sure your order contains full details of the goods required including catalogue or reference numbers (usually best tabulated as in the example above), as well as any terms agreed, delivery date (if agreed), any special conditions relating to the method of transport to be used, delivery address (if not clear from letterheading), etc.

Letter of acknowledgement of order

Universal Products Limited
Crown House
Marshall Street
SOUTHWARE
Middlesex
YT6 4RV

Your ref LM 21320
Our ref 982/jp

16 July 19 -

D Damion Esq
Fitzroy Motors Limited
151-153 Deanly Street
LONDON
SW1 EQ2

Dear Mr Damion

Thank you very much for your order no 23496, dated 12 July.

The order is receiving our immediate attention and will be despatched to you by the end of this week.

I hope we may continue to receive your valued custom.

Yours sincerely

John Jones
Managing Director

Letter from a supplier to a distributor requesting references

Marston Metal Supplies
Long Lane
MARSTON
Northants
LB7 9IN

Your ref PJ/M/69
Our ref JPQ/7/82

4 July 19 -

Peter Jones Esq
Managing Director
Maxi Components Limited
LECHFORD
Bucks
SL8 9IV

Dear Mr Jones

Thank you for your order of 28 June, which is receiving our prompt attention.

Since this is the first occasion on which you have placed an order with us, we would be grateful if you could furnish us with your banker's or a trade reference. Alternatively we would be happy to receive your remittance before despatch of your order.

Yours sincerely
Marston Metal Supplies

Peter Wood

Letter from a distributor to a supplier regarding request for a reference

Maxi Components Limited
LECHFORD
Bucks
SL8 9IV

Your ref JPQ/7/82
Our ref PJ/S/70

8 July 19 -

Mr Peter Wood
Marston Metal Supplies
Long Lane
MARSTON
Northants
LB7 9IN

Dear Mr Wood

Thank you for your letter of 4 July. Please contact either our branch of Midwest Bank plc, or Sankey Smith & Co, for the reference you require. Their addresses are as follows:

Mr John Wilson (Manager)
Midwest Bank plc
The Parade
LECHFORD
Bucks
SL8 8RT

Sankey Smith & Co Ltd
Unit 4
Beechfield Trading Estate
WALTON
Lancs
NR4 6BW

Yours sincerely

Peter Jones

Letter from a supplier taking up a trade reference

Marston Metal Supplies
Long Lane
MARSTON
Northants
LB7 9IN

13 July 19 -

Sankey Smith & Co Ltd
Unit 4
Beechfield Trading Estate
WALTON
Lancs
NR4 6BW

Dear Sirs

We have received an order for the sum of £-- from Maxi Components Limited of Lechford.

This is the first instance of our trading with this company, who have supplied your name for a trade reference. Please let us know, in confidence, whether or not this company has always regularly settled its accounts with you.

Yours faithfully
Marston Metal Supplies

Peter Wood

Letter to supplier from trade referee

Sankey Smith & Co Ltd
Unit 4
Beechfield Trading Estate
WALTON
Lancs
NR4 6BW

17 July 19 -

CONFIDENTIAL

Mr Peter Wood
Marston Metal Supplies
Long Lane
MARSTON
Northants
LB7 9IN

Dear Mr Wood

In reply to your letter of 13 July we can confirm that Maxi
Components Ltd have held an account with us for six years and
have always settled promptly. To the best of our knowledge
their financial and trading position is sound.

We would consider that there would be no problems in allowing
the company credit of the sum you mention.

Yours sincerely

Charles Seymour
Financial Director

Letter from a supplier to a distributor regarding references

Marston Metal Supplies
Long Lane
MARSTON
Northants
LB7 9IN

Your ref PJ/M/69
Our ref JPQ/7/82

23 July 19 -

Peter Jones Esq
Managing Director
Maxi Components Ltd
LECHFORD
Bucks
SL8 9IV

Dear Mr Jones

We are pleased to inform you that we are able to open an account for you, and can allow you credit up to £--. Our terms are 30 days nett from date of invoice.

We assure you of our prompt attention at all times.

Yours sincerely
Marston Metal Supplies

Peter Wood

Letter apologising for inability to supply goods/services

Marston Metal Supplies
Long Lane
MARSTON
Northants
LB7 9IN

Your ref PJ/M/69
Our ref JPQ/7/82

4 July 19 -

Peter Jones Esq
Managing Director
Maxi Components Limited
LECHFORD
Bucks
SL8 9IV

Dear Sir

Thank you for your order of 28 June. Unfortunately we are no longer able to supply the black anodised aluminium you require, due to the introduction of new government safety regulations concerning the use of chemicals involved in the anodising process. May I refer you, however, to National Metallic Limited, Southfields Way, Broton, Yorks NW2 7DX, who import a similar product which does not infringe the government safety regulations.

I apologise for this inconvenience, and hope that we may continue to supply your other aluminium requirements.

Yours faithfully
Marston Metal Supplies

Annette Wood

Letter complaining about late delivery of goods

8 Birchfield Drive
ACTONBURY ABBAS
Dorset
DN4 3DD

28 October 19 -

Countryways Fashion Wear Ltd
Countryways House
North Temple Street
LEEDS
LN6 1RR

Dear Sirs

On 16 September I sent you an order for a pair of 'Elegant Rider' fashion boots, together with a cheque for £42.00. These boots have not yet arrived and, since your advertisement states one should allow 28 days for delivery, I would be pleased if you would send my order immediately.

If there has been a delay in obtaining my size or preferred colours, it would have been a courtesy to inform me. Further, I know that my order has been received since my cheque has been cashed.

I look forward to either an explanation as to the delay, or my goods, by return of post.

Yours faithfully

Caroline Lockwood

Letter complaining about faulty goods (not returned)

8 Birchfield Drive
ACTONBURY ABBAS
Dorset
DN4 3DD

9 November 19 -

Countryways Fashion Wear Ltd
Countryways House
North Temple Street
LEEDS
LN6 1RR

Dear Sirs

I recently received a pair of your 'Elegant Rider' fashion boots through mail order. However, I am afraid to say that they are faulty. Whilst one boot is perfect, the other has no stitching around the back of the heel. Since the heel support is glued and then stitched, the one on this particular boot would quickly pull away.

Shall I send the boots back to you for replacement, or do you have a local stockist to whom I may take them for replacement? If I return them to you, no doubt you will refund the cost of the postage and packing?

I look forward to your reply.

Yours faithfully

Caroline Lockwood

It is usually best to write to a supplier expressing your dissatisfaction before returning goods. However, this letter could be adapted to accompany returned faulty goods.

Letter from supplier apologising about faulty goods

Countryways Fashion Wear Ltd
Countryways House
North Temple Street
LEEDS
LN6 1RR

13 November 19 -

Ms Caroline Lockwood
8 Birchfield Drive
ACTONBURY ABBAS
Dorset
DN4 3DD

Dear Ms Lockwood

We were very sorry to hear that the pair of boots we sent to you recently were imperfect.

We will of course replace the boots and would ask you to return them to us by parcel post. We enclose a prepaid lable to cover your postage.

Yours sincerely
for Countryways Fashion Wear

Martin Jones
Sales Director

Letter returning mail order goods (not faulty, but unsuitable)

7 Wheeler Street
COLBURN
Surrey
S9 7FD

26 May 19 -

Chrome Mail Order Co Ltd
Chrome House
19-31 Frank Road
LONDON
N22 6WK

Dear Sir

ORDER NO AS536

I am returning to you the shoes (cat no 83, size 5) which I ordered on 8 May and received on 23 May. Unfortunately, on closer inspection I found that they were not exactly the colour I need.

Since I am returning these goods within the period of your money-back guarantee, I look forward to receiving a cheque for £20 from you.

Yours faithfully

A J Smith (Ms)

Letter returning unsolicited goods

26 Horn Lane
BEARSFORD
Cornwall
C7 3UD

5 May 19 -

Crown Audio Co Ltd
24-30 Crewe Road
LONDON
N7 5DS

Dear Sir

INVOICE NO R978

I received a cassette, an invoice and some order forms from you yesterday through the post. Since I neither ordered nor require this cassette, I have no intention of paying for it.

If you wish to recover this property you should write to me to arrange a mutually convenient time for someone from your company to pick it up within the next month.

Please note that I do not wish to receive any more unsolicited goods.

Yours faithfully

A G Jones

Letter to shop regarding goods turning out to be faulty

Compton House
6 Fern Lane
FAIRFORD
Essex
E8 6TY

5 October 19 -

The Manager
Comfort Home Furniture
51-53 High Road
FAIRFORD
Essex
E9 7ES

Dear Sir

RECEIPT NO R635

I bought a sofa (Highfield, no 87) from your shop on 2 April 19 -.
Although it has certainly not received more than normal wear
and tear, it collapsed yesterday. It looks to me as though it is
broken beyond repair.

I would be grateful if you would arrange for it to be taken away
and inspected as soon as possible.

If you agree that it is irreparable, I will require either an identical
replacement or a refund.

I trust that you will give this matter your urgent attention.

Yours faithfully

David Miles

Circular letter (mailing shot) offering goods/services

Brown's Motor Repair Company
Brighton Road
COLBRIDGE
Sussex
RT5 7YH

Tel 0393 76567

April 19 -

Dear

If you drive a car then we think we can help you.

With our up-to-the-minute equipment and a team of experienced motor engineers we can service your car to keep it in tip-top condition, and can carry out all engine and body work repairs.

MOT tests can be carried out while you wait, with no need to make an appointment.

If we need more than three days to repair your car we will supply you with another vehicle at highly competitive rates, and give you a full tank of petrol — FREE.

For your added convenience our engineers can also visit your home and solve many of those annoying little problems without you even going outside your own front door.

So, if your car isn't quite perfect — or even if it is and you want to keep it that way — just pick up your 'phone. Any of our staff will be delighted to help you.

Yours sincerely

James Brown
Managing Director

If a mailing shot is designed to look like a personal letter, take the trouble to find out the names of your potential clients, and fill in their names. Such letters should also be personally signed.

Circular letter about a new branch of a business

DIY Supplies
10 The Parade
SOUTH WOODHAM
Merseyside
L17 5GJ

June 19 -

Dear Customer

NOW ITS EVEN EASIER TO GET THAT DIY JOB DONE!

We are pleased to report that demand for our 'do-it-yourself' tools and materials has increased so much that we are shortly to open a second branch on Merseyside.

The shop, at 14 Pinter Street, Fleetways, will stock all our usual ranges and will be under the management of Mr Brian Ampter. We open for business on 14 June, and to encourage both our old and new customers we will be offering a 5% discount on cash sales over £15 during the first two weeks of business.

We hope that the opening of this new branch will make it even more convenient for you to stock up on your DIY needs. Brian Ampter and his staff will be delighted to help you when you call.

Yours faithfully

Frank Green
Regional Director — DIY Supplies

Letter requesting service to central heating

4 Apley Way
BORDERTON
Lincs
LP4 4DL

16 September 19 -

Lincoln Gas
4 Dover Street
LINCOLN
LP4 6DG

Dear Sirs

We would like to have our central heating system serviced under the special 'parts only' plan advertised in the *Lincoln Post*. Our system is a Drayton 660.

There will be someone at home, each afternoon, after 2 pm.

Yours faithfully

A Barkworth

Similar letters can be used to request service to washing machines, televisions, etc. Stating the model number of the appliance in question can often mean quicker service.

Letter complaining about service

21 Plum Road
LONDON
SW3 8YT

14 August 19 -

The Manager
Horns Ltd
23-37 Fairbridge Road
LONDON
EC1 3SD

Dear Sir

INVOICE NO B512

I am writing to complain about the standard of servicing offered by your Company, and about the above invoice.

I notified your Service Department on 20 June in writing that my washing machine needed repairing. Your service engineers have since been four times — on 11 July, 18 July, 26 July and 6 August. The fault was diagnosed on the first visit and the wrong replacement part was brought by different engineers on the two subsequent visits. The correct part was fitted by the original engineer on the fourth visit.

In summary, my complaints are:
1   I had to wait three weeks for an engineer to call and nearly two months for the machine to be repaired;
2   the engineers who called on 18 and 26 July had been given inadequate or wrong information by the Company, which resulted in my taking two half days off work unnecessarily;
3   the first and fourth visits lasted a total of 30 minutes. In the above invoice, I have been charged 4 hours labour for four visits. I do not intend to pay your Company for their mistakes. Indeed, I feel it would be more appropriate if the Company offered to compensate me for the day's pay I lost through their mistake.

Therefore, I will not be paying the above invoice and look forward to receiving your response to these criticisms.

Yours faithfully

Robert Wallis

MONEY MATTERS

Letters concerning money matters should always be written in a clear and precise manner. It is best to avoid archaic phrases which your reader may misunderstand, and to write in concise sentences which leave no possibility of ambiguity.

When writing letters to a firm or financial institution it is best to address a particular individual. If you cannot find out the name of the appropriate person, at least make sure that your letter goes to the correct department. Within large organisations, and some smaller ones, too, it can take some time for a letter to arrive on the desk of the person who can deal with it if it arrives in the post room bearing no name.

Just as with any non-personal letter, those concerning money should never be rude — even if you are angry. State the subject matter of the letter in your first paragraph, and follow through the other points you want to make in a logical order. By sticking entirely to the facts in this way, you will put your case with the least likelihood of misunderstanding or offence.

Quite often it may be helpful to enclose relevant documents such as receipts. If you do this, always send copies, not the original, and say what you have enclosed in the text of your letter. To avoid any possible difficulties at a later stage it is wisest to keep a copy of any letter you write on a financial matter.

Lastly, always quote any reference given on a letter to which you are replying. Even if you do not use references yourself they will help your correspondent and thus speed up the handling of your business.

Raising invoices, statements, etc

Drafting statements and invoices

Most statements and invoices are issued by businesses who will have them printed in accordance with the legal requirements of the tax authorities. The full details of these requirements are beyond the scope of this book, and anyone wishing to issue invoices in the course of regular business should certainly seek the advice of HM Customs and Excise and a qualified accountant. Briefly, however, the following details should be set out clearly on any invoice or statement:

1   Your own name and address (and VAT registration number if you have one).

2   The date on which the goods or services were supplied.

3   A description which is sufficient to identify the goods or services which you have supplied.

4 The total amount payable, excluding any VAT.
5 Any cash discount.
6 The total amount of any VAT.
7 The customer's name (or trading name) and address.
8 The type of supply, such as sale, hire purchase, rental, exchange, etc. Points 7 and 8 can be omitted by retailers selling direct to the general public. Points 4 and 6 can also be replaced by a VAT inclusive price subject to prevailing limits on the sum payable.

A statement should give your name or trading name, the date of the statement and the dates, sums and numbers of all the transactions included on it. A statement should also make clear which of the invoices on it have been paid and what total sum remains owing at the statement date.

Example of an invoice

Invoice No 76

To A P Smith & Sons
    48 Arbroath Road
    LONDON
    NW8 6LR

14 July 19 -

Tax point 14 July 19 -

From   Motor Traders (UK) Limited
       Bowater Street
       YORK
       SL8 9RP   VAT Regd No 582 6543 21
Sale

Quantity	Description	Price Excluding VAT	VAT at 15%
1	Exhaust pipe	£50	£ 7.50
2	Brackets at £10	£20	£ 3.00
		£70	£ 10.50

Terms: Cash discount of 5% if paid within 14 days   Total £80.50

Example of a statement

AUTO MOTORS UK LIMITED   STATEMENT

Please send payment direct to Accounts Office: 58 Ebury Street
                                               MANCHESTER
                                               LM8 6AT
                                               Tel 061 898 4567

Lewis Spares
6-8 West Road
HIGH WYCOMBE
Buckinghamshire
SL7 5RQ

10 February 19 -

Date of Sale	Reference	Amount	
08/01/85	42002 CSH	27.95	INV - invoice
15/01/85	42069 INV	9.82	C/N - credit
31/01/85	42098 INV	3.40	CSH - cash
05/02/85	42121 INV	16.84	received
Balance outstanding £2.11			

Credit and debit notes

Credit notes are used to cancel or correct invoices and would be provided by a supplier to a buyer. They are also used for crediting goods returned to the supplier.

Credit notes are often typed in red, and should include details of:

1   Your own name and address.
2   Credit note number.
3   Your VAT registration number (if applicable).
4   Date.
5   Buyer's name and address.

and then, often tabulated:
original order or invoice number and date; reason for credit (eg overcharge, against return of faulty goods); amount credited; and, if applicable, the amount of VAT credited.

A debit note is used for correcting invoices which have been undercharged. It would include similar details to those on a credit note, but would be typed in black.

Example of a credit note

Credit Note No 32

Motor Traders (UK) Limited
Bowater Street
YORK
SL8 9RP

VAT Regd No 582 6543 21   8 August 19 -

To APP Smith & Sons
48 Arbroath Road
LONDON
NW8 6LR

Original Invoice No/date	Description	Credit excluding VAT	VAT	
			Rate	Amount
No 76 14 July 19 -	Returned exhaust bracket (faulty)	£10.00	15%	£3.00
Totals		£10.00		£3.00
Total amount credited		£13.00		

Receipt for money

34 Chelsea Walk
PETERBURGH
Lincs
PB8 2GT

Received from Richard Shipman, the sum of one hundred and
seventy five pounds only, in payment for the Mini van
(registration number NYO 252R) delivered to him on 3 April 19 -.

£175

Brian Hicks
3 April 19 -

Joint promissory note

63 Westerham Road
BROUGHTON
Sussex
LU9 6TV

26 February 19 -

£500

Six months after date, we promise to pay Napley Timber Limited, or order, the sum of Five Hundred Pounds sterling for value received.

Frank Hunter
James Fleming

Settlement of bills
Letter requesting settlement of an account

Napley Timber Limited
Walter's Yard
BROUGHTON
Sussex
LU7 5TN

6 February 19 -

F Hunter Esq
63 Westerham Road
BROUGHTON
Sussex
LU9 6TV

Dear Mr Hunter

We would much appreciate your immediate payment for the timber supplied to you during October and November 19 -.

We are now preparing our books for auditing and the delay in receiving your settlement is causing some inconvenience.

A duplicate statement is enclosed.

Yours sincerely
Napley Timber Limited

Brian Kent

Letter demanding settlement of an account

Napley Timber Limited
Walter's Yard
BROUGHTON
Sussex
LU7 5TN

15 February 19 -

F Hunter Esq
63 Westerham Road
BROUGHTON
Sussex
LU9 6TV

Dear Mr Hunter

We regret to note that your account for timber supplied during October and November 19 - is still outstanding. We wrote to you on 6 February enclosing a duplicate statement to serve as a reminder.

In these circumstances, I am afraid that unless we receive settlement within seven working days of the date of this letter I shall be forced to instruct our solicitors to take action.

Yours sincerely
Napley Timber Limited

Peter Harvey
Managing Director

A letter threatening proceedings should never be written unless you really feel that no other course remains open and you are prepared to carry through your threat. If circumstances do demand that such a letter be sent, it is sensible to send it by recorded delivery.

Letter advising of money remitted and requesting a receipt

19 Trehurst Crescent
BUXTON
Kent
MO5 2LR

6 August 19 -

Messrs Abbot and Coles
104 Smith Street
LONDON
SE21 6AJ

Dear Sirs

I enclose a cheque for £238.56, in full settlement of your invoice number 6583.

Please send me a receipt for this sum.

Yours faithfully

Ann Woods (Mrs)

Enc

Letter pointing out an overcharge in an invoice

19 Baverstock Avenue
READING
Berks
HY5 1SC

1 December 19 -

Accounts Department
Sportsman's Aid Limited
Sporting House
Myers Industrial Estate
LUDLEY
Wilts
YT7 4XT

Dear Sirs

I have this morning received your invoice dated 25 November.

As you will see, the second item is for two dozen X6 golf balls, at a total cost of £24. These were on my original order, but were cancelled in writing on 15 November. I must assume that you received this cancellation, since the balls were not included in my delivery.

I am returning your invoice and when it has been amended I shall be pleased to send you my cheque.

Yours faithfully

Michael Garfield

Enc

Do not forget to enclose the invoice. A similar letter could be sent about a mistake found in a statement.

Letter replying to a creditor

63 Westerham Road
BROUGHTON
Sussex
LU9 6TV

18 February 19 -

P Harvey Esq
Managing Director
Napley Timber Limited
Walter's Yard
BROUGHTON
Sussex
LU7 5TN

Dear Mr Harvey

I have this morning received your warning of legal proceedings in connection with my outstanding account. I am extremely sorry that you should feel such a step necessary, and no less sorry that I should have been the cause of it.

Since I have been a customer of yours for more than five years, and have settled my account promptly each month throughout that time, I trust that you may reconsider the matter. I have to admit that my finances have been strained recently, due to various unexpected extra costs. However, I confidently expect to return to a more solid basis next month and would be happy to issue a promissory note for the sum involved plus any reasonable interest.

I hope that you will accept this offer, and my apologies for the inconvenience I have caused.

Yours sincerely

Frank Hunter

When requesting a business favour this more personal sytle of letter can be successfully used. However, it should be used with caution if you do not know your correspondent personally, since it could appear presumptuous.

Letter requesting a statement of account

14 Alloa Road
NEWINGTON
Kent
LR5 7VN

9 August 19 -

Accounts Department
Messrs Perkin and Lambton
Orbit House
STONELEY
Middlesex
ST7 4RV

Dear Sirs

I should be most grateful if you would send me your statement of account up to and including 31 July 19 -.

Yours faithfully

Miles Sproggins

Letter to a shop asking why a request for hire purchase was refused

308 Cumber Road
LONDON
NW5 6LM

21 January 19 -

The Manager
Maybrick Stores
108 Pinder Street
LONDON
W1A 2AB

Dear Sir

I am writing to ask why I have been refused credit by your company.

On 18 January I came to your shop in order to buy a Hotflow 6X washing machine and a Hotflow Senior tumble drier, at a total cost of £634. Knowing from leaflets displayed within the store that you make credit facilities available to your customers I asked for the necessary paperwork to be prepared. I was most shocked when the assistant informed me that I could not have any credit, a decision confirmed by the Department Manager, Mr Smith.

I would appreciate your explanation of this refusal, which has caused me considerable inconvenience and embarrassment.

Yours faithfully

Andrew Blackstock

Under the Consumer Credit Act, traders and finance companies are not obliged to explain why they refuse to give a person credit, but they must tell you if they have used a credit reference agency provided you ask for this information, in writing, within a month of their refusing you credit.

Letter to credit reference agency asking for your personal file

308 Cumber Road
LONDON
NW5 6LM

5 February 19 -

Black and Company
Credit House
COMLEY
Berks
RP6 8SJ

Dear Sir

I understand from Mr A Mathews, the manager of Maybrick Stores, Pinder Street, London, that you are holding a file relating to my credit status. Since I have been refused credit by Maybrick Stores I must assume that the information you have about me, which you supplied to them, is unfavourable.

I wish to see a copy of any information you have about my financial affairs, and I enclose a postal order for £1 which I understand to be the appropriate handling charge.

Yours faithfully

Andrew Blackstock

Enc

You are entitled by law to see and correct any information wrongly held on files about you by a credit reference agency. Any corrections must be passed on to anyone who has been given a reference on you in the last six months.

Letter to hire purchase company advising of difficulty in meeting repayments

3 Seacombe Villas
Archery Fields
ARDEN
Kent
KJ7 6TB

6 May 19 -

Southern Credit Company
12-14 Arlington Street
LONDON
SW1 6HL

Dear Sir

AGREEMENT HP23/64/82

I am having some difficulty in meeting the repayments for the car that I am buying in accordance with the terms of the above agreement. The contract was signed on 12 August 19 -, and since then I have paid regularly each month. Unfortunately I now find that my commitments are more than my financial situation will stand.

I have no wish to default on my debt to your company, and would therefore much appreciate it if you would consider allowing me to make rather smaller payments over a longer period.

I would be most grateful if you could let me know whether such an arrangement is possible and, if so, what the new terms would be.

Yours faithfully

Peter Smithson

As with any debt about which there is some difficulty, it is advisable to write to the creditor and make whatever realistic offer you can.

Banks and building societies

Letter to bank requesting working overdraft

51 Church Street
ROYBURN
Berkshire
6XJ 9PQ

10 March 19 -

E R Cox Esq
The Manager
London and District Bank
119 Bolton Street
ROYBURN
Berkshire
6YN 5FV

Dear Mr Cox

ACCOUNT NO 55376426

I am writing to enquire about the possibility of having a monthly working overdraft of £500.

As you will see from my file, I am self-employed in an industry renowned for the slowness by which invoices are settled. This results in my account being somewhat overdrawn at the beginning of each month, although the position regularises itself as the month progresses.

I would of course be happy to come and discuss this matter with you at any convenient time.

Yours sincerely

Simon Dennis

This letter can be adapted for an individual writing to the bank for a temporary overdraft necessitated by unexpected financial outlays due to car repairs, holidays, etc.

Letter to bank confirming that a cheque should be stopped

51 Church Street
ROYBURN
Berks
6XJ 9PQ

10 July 19 -

The Manager
London and District Bank
119 Bolton Street
ROYBURN
Berks
6YN 5FV

Dear Sir

This is to confirm my telephone call of this morning asking you to stop payment of my cheque number 4248 638, dated 4 July 19-. It was for the sum of £586 and was signed by me in favour of Mr Eric Palfrey.

Mr Palfrey has not received the cheque and I must therefore assume that it has been lost in the post.

Yours faithfully

Simon Dennis

Only stop a cheque for a good reason, such as that it has been lost or that fraud is suspected.

Letter (general) confirming loss of cheque card/cheque book

51 Church Street
ROYBURN
Berks
6XJ 9PQ

10 May 19 -

E R Cox Esq
The Manager
London and District Bank
119 Bolton Street
ROYBURN
Berks
6YN 5FV

Dear Mr Cox

I am writing to confirm my telephone call of this morning, in which I informed a member of your staff, Miss Jones, that I have lost my cheque card, Number 456789.

I first noticed the loss of my card this morning, and I know that it was in my wallet on 8 May when I used it to cash my cheque Number 12345 at your High Street branch.

Yours sincerely

Simon Dennis

Letter to building society advising of difficulty in paying mortgage due to redundancy

6 Amberley Villas
BURCHFORD
Oxon
LM9 6PR

1 April 19 -

The Manager
Midlands Building Society
Abbey House
Upper High Road
GLOSTER
Oxon
LM8 9AB

Dear Sir

MORTGAGE POLICY NUMBER 898/LMR/63

I am afraid I must write to inform you that I am having considerable difficulty in meeting my mortgage repayments, and can foresee no immediate improvement in my financial situation.

My employers for the last fifteen years, J M Smith and Company, went into liquidation in January and I was therefore made redundant. I am of course actively seeking another position, but as you will appreciate employment is not easy to find at present in this area.

I have some savings in addition to my redundancy payment, but despite cutting back on many fronts I am finding it hard to meet all my commitments. It would cause great upset for my family if we were forced to move house, and I wondered therefore if I might be allowed to reduce my monthly payments by 20% for the present, extending the total length of my mortgage to compensate for this? After careful consideration I am certain that I could meet the interest payment regularly, and I very much hope that you will give your sympathetic consideration to my situation.

I would naturally be happy to come and discuss this matter further with you if you feel it would be helpful.

Yours faithfully

Malcolm Jones

Insurance

Letter to insurance company notifying of death

6 Crane Drive
BROMLEY
Cornwall
C7 8YT

30 June 19 -

Trust Insurance Co Ltd
69 Croft Lane
LONDON
EC1 6DR

Dear Sirs

TRUST INSURANCE POLICY NO 6781

The holder of the above policy, Gerald Young, died on 28 June.

As executor of his will, I would be grateful if you would inform
me of the amount of money the beneficiary will receive, and
when you expect to pay this sum. Please also confirm that the
beneficiary named is still Mrs G Young.

Yours faithfully

Andrew Blake

Letter to insurance company advising of theft

Pigeon Cottage
Flight Hill
BANWOOD
Oxon
SL8 5NM

21 May 19 -

Reliant Insurance Company Limited
Pimlico Street
LONDON
SW1 6XJ

Dear Sir

POLICY NUMBER LM 169380

I am writing to report that a theft occurred at the above address on the night of 19 May 19 -

My wife and I were both at home on the night in question, but knew nothing of the theft until 7.30 am on the morning of 20 May, when I realised that the kitchen window was open. We quickly discovered that various items were missing, and telephoned the police. I have made a full statement to the police at Banwood Police Station, where Detective Inspector Charles is in charge of the case.

I enclose a full list of the items that are missing, with their replacement values. Fortunately nothing irreplaceable was taken and I have been able to confirm the values quite easily.

I will willingly give you any further information that may be helpful, and hope that a settlement can be made without delay.

Yours faithfully

Barry Spinks

Enc

Always inform your insurance company of any claim immediately, even if you do not yet know the extent of the loss. Most companies will then send you a claim form to fill in, which would take the place of the list sent with the above sample letter.

The letter could be adapted for a case of accidental damage to insured goods.

104

Letter to insurance company in respect of a car accident when it is not your fault

60 Waldemar
Avenue
LONDON
NW6 6LR

29 June 19 -

Resteasy Insurance Company
Resteasy House
LUTTON
Surrey
FT5 7YB

Dear Sirs

POLICY NUMBER 687 LM 982 Z

I have to report that this evening, whilst I was driving down Maida Vale, a van overtook me and badly scraped the side of my car.

The accident was, on his own admission, entirely the fault of the other driver. His name is Ian Morton and he is an employee of Coast Deliveries (6 Oak Court, London, SE16 2XN) whose van he was driving at the time. Since no one was injured in any way, and the cause of the accident was not in dispute, the police were not called. However, a Mrs Ann Wood, of 16 Arley Road, London, N8 4SP, saw the incident clearly and has given me permission to mention her name should an independent witness be called for.

I have not yet obtained estimates for the repairs needed, but will forward them to you in the next few days.

Yours faithfully

James Sudbury

ACCOMMODATION

Landlord and tenant

When there is a query or dispute between a landlord and his tenant, it is wise for both parties to put their point of view formally in a letter. If the letters are clearly written they may themselves help to clear up any misunderstandings, and an amicable solution be facilitated. If the problem is more deep seated, it is possible that legal steps may follow from one side or the other, and if this happens it will be much quicker and cheaper for everybody concerned if the points of view have been clearly stated at an early stage.

Just as for any other business letter, make sure that you acknowledge any letter you are answering, and reply to the questions it raised. State all the relevant facts and put your points firmly, but whatever your feelings may be it will never be helpful to become abusive — indeed, written abuse can lead to serious trouble.

Letter from a landlord to a tenant, reminding him that the rent is overdue

40 Moreley Drive
POOLFORD
Dorset
JP8 6YB

21 May 19 -

Mr Peter Smith
94 Court Road
POOLFORD
Dorset
JO9 5TB

Dear Mr Smith

May I remind you that the rent due from you on 30 April for the property you occupy at 94 Court Road, has not yet been received.

I would be grateful for your remittance as soon as possible.

Yours sincerely

Ian Graham

This letter could be followed up, if necessary, by a more strongly worded letter. However, as with letters concerning buying and selling goods, do not threaten legal action unless you mean to follow it through.

Letter of reply to a landlord requesting overdue rent

94 Court Road
POOLFORD
Dorset
JO9 5TB

24 May 19 -

Ian Graham Esq
40 Moreley Drive
POOLFORD
Dorset
JP8 6YB

Dear Mr Graham

I am very sorry that you have had to write to me requesting payment of my rent, which I know is overdue.

The last three months have been very difficult for me since I was made redundant. However, I have now started work again and with a regular wage I will try to pay off my debt to you as quickly as possible. Would you agree to my paying an extra £12 per month until the backlog is cleared?

I realise now that I should have explained the situation to you sooner, and hope that you will accept my apologies.

Yours sincerely

Peter Smith

Letter from a landlord raising the rent of tenant

40 Moreley Drive
POOLFORD
Dorset
JP8 6YB

12 May 19 -

Mr Peter Smith
94 Court Road
POOLFORD
Dorset
JO9 5TB

Dear Mr Smith

I am writing to give you formal notice that, as from 25 June 19 -, your rent will be increased from £30 to £35 per week.

I am forced to take this step owing to the recent increase in rates.

Yours sincerely

Ian Graham

Send a formal notification such as this by registered post, keeping the receipt, to avoid any dispute as to delivery. If there is a tenancy agreement the landlord should make sure to give the proper amount of notice of any rent increase.

Letter from a landlord to an outgoing tenant asking the latter to allow a prospective tenant to see over the house

40 Moreley Drive
POOLFORD
Dorset
JP8 6YB

1 October 19 -

Mr Peter Smith
94 Court Road
POOLFORD
Dorset
JO9 5TB

Dear Mr Smith

As your tenancy expires at the end of this month, may I ask if you would allow a prospective tenant to look over the house?

I should be most grateful if you would permit this. Naturally the person concerned would only come by appointment, at a time convenient to Mrs Smith and yourself.

Yours sincerely

Ian Graham

Letter from a landlord serving notice to quit on a tenant

40 Moreley Drive
POOLFORD
Dorset
JP8 6YB

12 June 19 -

Mr Peter Smith
94 Court Road
POOLFORD
Dorset
JO9 5TB

Dear Mr Smith

Since I have not received any rent from you since 30 March for the property you occupy at 94 Court Road, I am now forced to give you formal notice to leave. In accordance with your tenancy agreement I am giving you two weeks' notice from the date of this letter.

Yours sincerely

Ian Graham

Letter from a tenant asking for an extension of time to pay the rent

94 Court Road
POOLFORD
Dorset
JO9 5TB

16 May 19 -

Ian Graham Esq
40 Moreley Drive
Poolford
DORSET
JP8 6YB

Dear Mr Graham

I am writing to ask whether you would be kind enough to allow me an extension of time in which to pay my rent on the above property?

I recently suffered an accident which has meant that I have been away from work for six weeks. As a result I have been very short of money. I am returning to work on Monday 20 May and will therefore soon be able to get my finances on a sound footing once more. I would be most grateful if you could agree to my paying this month's rent in two instalments at the ends of June and July.

Yours sincerely

Peter Smith

In writing a letter such as this, always give the reason why you need an extension of time to pay and suggest how you would like to pay your debts in order to reassure your landlord that he will get his money.

Letter from a tenant asking for a rent reduction

94 Court Road
POOLFORD
Dorset
JO9 5TB

12 May 19 -

Ian Graham Esq
40 Moreley Drive
POOLFORD
Dorset
JP8 6YB

Dear Mr Graham

I am writing to ask if you will agree to reduce the rent I am paying for the above house.

As you know, I have lived here for eight years now and have always kept the property in excellent repair. You will also know that I have done many repair jobs myself rather than trouble you to call in workmen.

The latest rent increase will cause me considerable financial hardship and means that I will be paying considerably more than any of my immediate neighbours. I realise that the house is in better condition and might therefore command a higher rent on the open market, but I am bound to say that I feel it is rather unfair to penalise a tenant who looks after your property particularly well.

I hope you will look favourably on this request.

Yours sincerely

Peter Smith

Letter from a landlord refusing to reduce the rent

40 Moreley Drive
POOLFORD
Dorset
JP8 6YB

16 May 19 -

Mr Peter Smith
94 Court Road
POOLFORD
Dorset
JO9 5TB

Dear Mr Smith

I regret that it is impossible for me to reduce the rent of your house.

I appreciate that you have always been an excellent tenant and have undertaken various minor repairs yourself. However, the cost of the major work to your roof last year and the recent rate increases mean that I cannot consider any rent reduction.

I cannot discuss the rents paid by your neighbours beyond saying that the outgoings on each of my properties are different, and each has to be considered individually.

Yours sincerely

Ian Graham

Letter to a landlord asking him to effect repairs

94 Court Road
POOLFORD
Dorset
JO9 5TB

25 May 19 -

Ian Graham Esq
40 Moreley Drive
POOLFORD
Dorset
JP8 6YB

Dear Mr Graham

During the last three days a large crack has developed in my dining room ceiling. Pieces of plaster have fallen off and additional hairline cracks are now appearing. I have been into the loft and can find no dampness or other obvious cause of the problem.

I should be most grateful if you would arrange for a builder to inspect the property as soon as possible since I fear that even more serious damage may occur.

Yours sincerely

Peter Smith

Letter to a tenant refusing to carry out repairs

40 Moreley Drive
POOLFORD
Dorset
JP8 6YB

12 August 19 -

Mr Peter Smith
94 Court Road
POOLFORD
Dorset
JO9 5TB

Dear Mr Smith

Thank you for your letter of 1 August, requesting repairs to be undertaken on your stairs. I am afraid, however, that it is quite impossible for me to consider paying for any such major repairs for some time.

During the last two years most of the rent has been absorbed by the various repairs and redecoration work, and the property has become a severe drain on my own income.

While I do not wish to seem unreasonable, I am forced to refuse your request.

Yours sincerely

Ian Graham

Letter to a landlord concerning recurring repairs

94 Court Road
POOLFORD
Dorset
JO9 5TB

18 May 19 -

Ian Graham Esq
40 Moreley Drive
POOLFORD
Dorset
JP8 6YB

Dear Mr Graham

I am afraid I must inform you that the window in our kitchen still cannot be opened more than five centimetres, despite the efforts of your workmen on 6 May.

I would very much appreciate it if you could arrange for a further attempt to be made to free it. As I am sure you will understand, my wife has been finding the kitchen less than fresh during the recent hot weather.

With many thanks for your attention in this matter.

Yours sincerely

Peter Smith

Letter to a landlord stronger in tone than the former

94 Court Road
POOLFORD
Dorset
JO9 5TB

25 May 19 -

Ian Graham Esq
40 Moreley Drive
POOLFORD
Dorset
JP8 6YB

Dear Mr Graham

KITCHEN AT 94 COURT ROAD

I am afraid that I feel I must write to you again about the state of our kitchen.

We received a visit from your building contractor, Mr Ady, on 14 May, when he promised to bring a new sink unit within one week. He also promised to repair the window the following day. Neither of these things has happened.

As you know, the sink unit was cracked to the extent of being unusable when we moved here on 1 April. The window has been attended to once already, but clearly without success since we are still unable to open it more than a few centimetres.

The hot weather recently has made the unventilated kitchen extremely unpleasant for my wife and children, and my wife is greatly inconvenienced by the lack of a sink.

I would appreciate your immediate attention to these matters.

Yours sincerely

Peter Smith

However justifiably angry you may feel, never threaten legal action or the involvement of sanitary inspectors or the like unless you really intend to carry out your threat.

Letter asking a landlord to release a tenant from tenancy before the lease has expired

94 Court Road
POOLFORD
Dorset
JO9 5TB

30 October 19 -

Mr Ian Graham
40 Moreley Drive
POOLFORD
Dorset
JP8 6YB

Dear Mr Graham

My husband has just accepted promotion to a new job near Bristol, and we are anxious to move into that area as soon as possible. I realise that our lease on this house still has three years to run, but I wonder if you would be so kind as to consider releasing us from the agreement before that time is up? If you can allow this, I would much appreciate your letting me know the date on which our tenancy could end, and the terms you would expect us to agree to.

If at all possible we would like to leave by the end of the year, and we will of course be ready to meet any reasonable terms you may offer. I am very sorry to put you to this trouble, and would like to take this opportunity of saying how much we have enjoyed living here.

Yours sincerely

Irene Smith (Mrs)

Letter from a landlord to an agent about early reoccupation

63 Oram Square
OXRIDGE
Oxon
6PJ 9TQ

23 July 19 -

Mr Brian Buckland
Buckland Ballard and Partners
15 New Street
LONDON
SW1 5PJ

Dear Brian Buckland

4 STANSWICK ROAD

Thank you for your letter of 3 July concerning the tenancy of 4 Stanswick Road. I would like new tenants found as soon as possible since, as you know, the financial loss involved in having an empty property is considerable.

Yours sincerely

Michael Brown

Letter to an agent concerning repairs

63 Oram Square
OXRIDGE
Oxon
6PJ 9TQ

23 July 19 -

Mr Brian Buckland
Buckland Ballard and Partners
15 New Street
LONDON
SW1 5PJ

Dear Brian Buckland

Thank you for your letter of 3 July regarding repairs to Nos 4 and 6 Stanswick Road.

Both roofs must of course be made good. Could you obtain three estimates and forward them to me for approval.

The request for a new sink unit in the kitchen of No 4 worries me a little. I see from my records that a new sink was installed only four years ago, for the same tenants. Could you visit the house and inspect the general condition in which the tenants are maintaining the property? I would appreciate your recommendation on the matter.

I shall be on holiday for four weeks from 10 August, and would like to settle all these matters before I go.

Yours sincerely

Michael Brown

Buying and selling a house

Letter to an estate agent regarding sale of house

32 Church Gardens
DUNHAM
Bucks
SB3 3DX

19 May 19 -

Miss M Wicks
Messrs Robinson & Whitlow
19-21 High Street
DUNHAM
Bucks
SBN 13D

Dear Miss Wicks

32 CHURCH GARDENS, DUNHAM, BUCKS

This is to confirm our agreement that your company will act as sole agents for the purchase of the above property at a commission rate of 1½% plus VAT. We understand that should we at any time decide to offer the house for sale through joint agency, then the commission rate due to your company will be

2% plus VAT assuming your company introduces an eventual purchaser.

We further confirm that the sale particulars you have supplied are satisfactory.

Yours sincerely

Robin Austin

Letter to a solicitor regarding sale of house

32 Church Gardens
DUNHAM
Bucks
SB3 3DX

16 May 19 -

Messrs Upley, Pope and Dykes
5-7 Broad Street
DUNHAM
Bucks
SB3 1BN

Dear Sirs

32 CHURCH GARDENS, DUNHAM, BUCKS

This is to confirm our conversation of 14 May with Mrs Williams of your office, whereby we agreed to your company handling the conveyancing arrangements both for the sale of 32 Church Gardens, Dunham, Bucks, and the purchase of New Farm, Chilton Matravers, Bucks. Your estimated fee was £750.00 plus VAT, stamp duty, land registration, searches and mortage costs.

The purchasers of 32 Church Gardens are:

Mr and Mrs S Boyer
16 Berry Close
Dunham
Bucks
SB3 5SN

The vendors of New Farm are:

Mr and Mrs R Chapman

Please let me know what further information you require in the form of mortgage account numbers, deeds, etc.

Yours faithfully

Robin Austin

Building work

Letter to a builder requesting an estimate

38 Ellerton Drive
COPLEY
Lancs
LNP 4DJ

Copley 61544

16 September 19 -

Messrs Stokeley & Wicks
   (Builders) Ltd
46 Winlow Lane
BRACKLEY
Lancs
LNP 1ST

Dear Sirs

Would you please come and give us a written estimate for some alterations we wish to have carried out.

Basically the work entails removing an adjoining wall between two rooms, sealing up one doorway, and altering the position of one of the radiators and the light switch.

We would like to have this work carried out within the next three months. Please telephone us at any time to arrange a visit.

Yours faithfully

George Wills

Letter to a builder accepting an estimate

38 Ellerton Drive
COPLEY
Lancs
LNP 4DJ

Your ref SW 63/GW

13 October, 19 -

Messrs Stokely & Wicks
  (Builders) Ltd
46 Winlow Lane
BRACKLEY
Lancs
LNP 1ST

Dear Sirs

This letter is to confirm our acceptance of your estimate dated 4 October, 19 -.

We also confirm that a commencing date of 3 November is satisfactory.

We look forward to seeing you then.

Yours faithfully

George Wills

Letter to a builder complaining about work carried out

38 Ellerton Drive
COPLEY
Lancs
LNP 4DJ

15 December 19 -

Your ref SW 63/aw

Messrs Stokeley & Wicks
   (Builders) Ltd
46 Winlow Lane
BRACKLEY
Lancs
LNP 1ST

Dear Sirs

You recently carried out some structural alterations and redecoration at our house, but I have to tell you that the work has proved to be most unsatisfactory.

Although initially all seemed to be fine, large cracks have appeared throughout the new plasterwork on the ceiling. Furthermore, moving the radiator has resulted in a constant leakage from the union with the pipework. No amount of tightening seems to cure this.

I would be grateful if you would come and rectify these problems as soon as possible since, apart from the unsightliness of the ceiling, it is impossible to use the radiator at present.

Yours faithfully

George Wills

Letters to local authorities

Letter to a rent officer about rent rebate

15 Albion Road
BLESSOP
Lancs
LR2 9PQ

15 July 19 -

The Rent Officer
Crown House
Queen Street
BLESSOP
Lancs
LR6 8UH

Dear Sir

I am writing to enquire about the possibility of receiving a rent rebate on my rental of the above property.

My total earnings, before tax, amount to approximately £140 per week, and no other member of my family is currently employed. Excluding rates, my weekly rent for our accommodation is £46. I have three children and am finding it hard to make ends meet, but it would be impossible for us to move to anywhere smaller since we already find our two bedrooms very cramped.

I would appreciate your advice on whether, and if so how, I may be able to get a rebate.

Yours faithfully

John Collins

Letter to Rent Tribunal about unfair rent

15 Albion Close
BLESSOP
Lancs
LR5 8UJ

15 July 19 -

Rent Tribunals
Crown House
Queen Street
BLESSOP
Lancs
LR6 8UH

Dear Sirs

I am writing to ask about the possibility of getting my rent
reduced.

I have been renting a two-bedroomed flat at the above address
for six years. We have our own kitchen and toilet, but we share
the bathroom, stairs and entrance hall with another family.

My earnings amount to approximately £130 per week, before
deductions, out of which I have to support two teenage sons.
My rent has recently been increased by £5 to £55 per week, and
this does not include any bills. In view of the poor state of repair
of the house this rent seems far too high, and I would be most
grateful if you could tell me how I may set about getting it
reduced.

Yours faithfully

Mary Stopps (Mrs)

Letter objecting to environmental nuisance

36A Rowner's Way
COPLEY
Sussex
SN3 1PJ

16 May 19 -

The Environmental Health Officer
Copley Borough Council
Municipal Buildings
High Street
COPLEY
Sussex
SN3 4PP

Dear Sir

I wish to complain about the early start being made by builders working on the flats in Spellthorne Park Road, which is only a few metres from our back garden.

For the last few days work has commenced as early as 5 am! Since they are laying bricks, you can imagine the noise. Surely such an early start cannot be permitted, for it is almost impossible to sleep once they have begun.

I would be most grateful if you could look into this matter as soon as possible, to ensure that work begins at a more reasonable time.

Yours faithfully

S J Carter

The importance of such a letter is to bring the matter to the attention of the relevant body, who will then deal with it. The letter can be modified to cover poor roads, smells, etc. Look under the entry for your council in your telephone directory for the relevant body to contact.

Letter enquiring about improvement grants

29 Cobble Lane
CUFFLEY
Cumbria
C9 6TR

16 November 19 -

The Home Improvements Officer
Cuffley Council
Cuffley Town Hall
26-38 High Road
CUFFLEY
Cumbria
C5 3PD

Dear Sir

I wish to install a toilet and bathroom in my house. At present it has no bathroom and an outside toilet.

I own the freehold of the house, which I bought 3 years ago. The house was built in 1898 and has a rateable value of £180.

I understand that there are various home improvement grants available. I would be grateful if you would advise me on whether I may be eligible for any of these and, if so, send me the relevant application form.

Yours faithfully

Alan Stevens

Letter asking for planning permission

8 Grey Lane
WESTER
Lancs
L3 9FG

9 March 19 -

The Planning Officer
Wester Council
32-34 Brick Road
WESTER
Lancs
L3 3JK

Dear Sir

I wish to extend my outhouse. I enclose drawings of the proposed alteration and I would be grateful if you would advise me on whether an application for planning permission is required for this modification.

If so, please send me the relevant form and give me an indication of the length of time it usually takes to process such an application.

Yours faithfully

Edward Cramer

Enc 3 drawings

If the proposed change is substantial, the writer need only ask for the form. The name of the officer and relevant department varies from council to council.

Letter objecting to planning permission

18 Whistler Road
BROCKFORD
Cheshire
C8 3UG

9 June 19 -

The Planning Officer
Brockford Council
Brockford Town Hall
218-240 Cross Road
BROCKFORD
Cheshire
C8 6FR

Dear Sir

APPLICATION FOR PLANNING PERMISSION NO 1987

I wish to object to the proposed extension for which the above application has been made.

Having viewed the plans, I am sure that this building, if constructed, would block off the light from my lower rooms and much of my back garden during the afternoon and evening.

Therefore, I request that you reject this application.

Yours faithfully

R Hancock (Ms)

MISCELLANEOUS

Appointments and travel
Letter making an appointment (general)

15 Lea Road
DALSTON
Surrey
PK8 5RG

17 August 19 -

Julian Boot Esq
Messrs Boot, Mather and Smith
12 City Chambers
LONDON
EC3 9ZX

Dear Mr Boot

I would like to make an appointment to discuss my will with you. Would the afternoon of Thursday 25 or Friday 26 August, be convenient? I am most anxious to settle matters as quickly as possible.

Yours sincerely

Timothy Bright

Letter confirming an appointment

Messrs Boot, Mather and Smith
12 City Chambers
LONDON
EC3 9ZX

Our ref BB/TB/82

19 August 19 -

Timothy Bright Esq
15 Lea Road
DALSTON
Surrey
PK8 5RG

Dear Mr Bright

Thank you for your letter of 17 August concerning the matter of your will.

I will be most happy to discuss it with you, and will expect you at 3.00 pm on Thursday 25 August.

Yours sincerely

Julian Boot

Letter cancelling/postponing an appointment

15 Lea Road
DALSTON
Surrey
PK8 5RG

Your ref BB/TB/82

23 August 19 -

Julian Boot Esq
Messrs Boot, Mather and Smith
12 City Chambers
LONDON
EC3 9ZX

Dear Mr Boot

I am very sorry to say that I shall not be able to keep our appointment on Thursday 25 August. An urgent family matter has arisen which means that I must be out of London until at least the end of the week.

I will telephone your secretary as soon as I return, to make an alternative arrangement.

I apologise for any inconvenience caused.

Yours sincerely

Timothy Bright

Letter to a hotel/guest house booking accommodation

97 Hamfirth Road
GOSHOLT
Avon
LXX 1PJ

16 March 19 -

The Manager
Sea View Hotel
The Promenade
WADLEY SANDS
Somerset
SM3 1T

Dear Sir

Further to our telephone booking of 15 March, this is to confirm that we would like a double room with sea view for six nights, arriving on 14 June and departing 20 June. We shall require full board.

I enclose a cheque for £20 deposit.

Yours faithfully

S M Parker

APPENDICES

Appendix A Use of English

If a business letter cannot be understood, because it is poorly written with disregard for the rules of grammar, it may well not achieve its purpose. The recipient of your letter may spend so much effort trying to sort out exactly what you mean by a particular sentence, he may forget the important point that you had just made or may lose track of the overall argument. So it is in order to avoid confusion and misunderstanding, as well as to give a good impression of yourself and your business, that you should try to write correctly.

Unfortunately for the average letter writer, language is a living entity and correct usage changes over the years. Furthermore, constructions which you may 'get away with' in daily conversation may not be grammatically acceptable in writing prose. The gap between what we 'get away with' in speech and what is correct in writing presents considerable difficulty to many people. The rules of English grammar are extremely complicated, but for the purposes of business letter writing it is sufficient to be familiar with the basic structure of a correct sentence and the rules of proper punctuation. If you know those, and avoid trying to write long and complex sentences, you should avoid many mistakes. Keep a dictionary beside you to check any spellings of which you are unsure, and be aware of the common pitfalls listed in this section.

There is only room to include the basic points of grammar here. Several more comprehensive books on the use of grammar are available.

The sentence

A sentence is defined as a group of words which make complete sense. In order to do this, it must contain two parts: the subject, a word or words about which the sentence will say something, and a predicate, a word or words about the subject. For example, in the sentence

The boy stole an apple.

The first part, the boy, is the subject, and the second part, stole an apple, is the predicate.

Note the following guidelines when writing a sentence:

1 Avoid splitting your subject and predicate.
   Do not write:

   David, after fighting with John at the park, repented.

   Write:

   After fighting with John at the park, David repented.

2 Avoid splitting an infinitive (to run, to walk, to obey, etc).
   Do not write:

   Peter wanted to carefully and meticulously stick the stamps in his album.

Write:
>
> Peter wanted to stick the stamps in his album carefully and meticulously.

3 Keep the same subject.

Do not write:
>
> We were cold at the seaside because one felt the wind.

Write:
>
> We were cold at the seaside because we felt the wind.

4 Keep the same tense.

Do not write:
>
> Jane answered the telephone but nobody speaks.

Write:
>
> Jane answered the telephone but nobody spoke.

Some grammatical pitfalls

1 Collective nouns

Collective nouns are nouns which are singular in form but refer to a group of persons or things. One must be careful to use a singular or a plural verb depending on the purpose of the particular sentence.

> The committee was furious with the plans for a strike.

That is, the committee was acting as a group.

> The committee were arguing among themselves over the plans for a strike.

That is, the committee were obviously acting as individuals, not as a unit.

2 Pronouns

The most common error involving pronouns is in phrases using 'me' and 'I'. For example, 'between you and I' should be 'between you and me'.

3 Adjectives

Similar to the problem of the collective noun is the problem of 'distributive' adjectives and pronouns. These are: anybody, nobody, everybody, either, neither, each, every, none. They are all singular, and must be used with verbs and pronouns in the singular.

Do not write:
>
> Everybody who travels abroad must have their passports.

Write:
>
> Everybody who travels abroad must have his passport.

And, do not write:
>
> Each of the children were given balloons after the party.

Write:
>
> Each of the children was given a balloon after the party.

4 Verbs

Verbs are singular or plural depending on the singular or plural nature of their subject.

(a) It is correct to write, either:
>
> Those dishes, left from Julie's party, have not been washed.

133

Or, to write:

That stack of dishes, left from Julie's party, has not been washed.

(b) The use of 'and', is like the plus sign in mathematics and makes a plural total.

John and Kathy were at the restaurant.

If we use any other words to join John and Kathy, this does not happen.

John, as well as his girlfriend Kathy, was at the restaurant.

5 Adverbs

The most common mistake here is to use an adjective when an adverb is required.

Do not write:

She ate the biscuits very quick.

Write:

She ate the biscuits very quickly.

6 Prepositions

(a) Avoid using the prepositional phrase 'due to' when 'because of' conveys the correct idea of causation.

Do not write:

The cricket match was stopped due to the rain.

Write:

The cricket match was stopped because of the rain.

(b) Avoid using the verb 'following' when prepositions and prepositional phrases such as 'after', 'because of', 'as a result of', and 'in accordance with', are more accurate.

Do not write:

Following the heavy rains, the roads flooded.

Write:

Because of the heavy rains, the roads flooded.

or

After the heavy rains, the roads flooded.

7 Miscellaneous errors

(a) Than

John is cleverer than me.

This is incorrect because the complete sentence would be:

John is cleverer than I am.

Write:

John is cleverer than I.

(b) Less and fewer

'Fewer' should be used when the persons or objects referred to can be counted, use 'less' when what is referred to cannot be counted.

Write:

James ate no fewer than four biscuits at tea.

James takes less sugar in his tea than I do.

The exception to this rule is in statements about time and distance.

London is less than 32 kilometres from our country cottage, and it should take less than an hour to get there.

Punctuation

The most commonly used punctuation marks in English are:

full stop	.
colon	:
semi-colon	;
comma	,
parentheses	( )
dash	—
question mark	?
exclamation mark	!
quotation marks	' '
apostrophe	'

1 Fullstop

Every declarative sentence must end with a fullstop.

2 Colon

The colon signals that an explanation or more information follows.

(a) It is used to introduce a series.

The child wanted three things for Christmas: a large stuffed animal, some coloured paper, and a small bicycle.

(b) It is used to introduce a quotation.

My mother's favourite saying is from Mark Twain: 'Work consists of whatever a body is obliged to do . . . Play consists of whatever a body is not obliged to do.'

(c) It is used to separate two clauses of equal weight.

Paul said it was time for supper: I said we had just finished lunch.

3 Semi-colon

This functions mainly in a long sentence to separate clauses where a pause between a comma and a fullstop is needed.

4 Comma

The comma is the most frequently used punctuation mark.

(a) It is used to separate items in a list of three or more words.

(b) It is used to separate phrases which depend on the same word.

I have travelled in Canada in a canoe, in Egypt on a camel, and in England on a train.

(c) It is used in a long sentence where a natural pause occurs.

5 Parentheses (sometimes known as brackets)

These are used in pairs when the writer has an interruption or aside not necessarily relevant to the main idea of the sentence.

6 Dash

A pair of dashes may be used to replace parentheses.

A single dash may be used in informal contexts to replace the colon in sentences such as 2(c).

Dashes should not be used as 'all purpose' punctuation marks.

7 Question mark

This is used at the end of a sentence which is a direct question.

Is there any milk on the doorstep?

Do not use for an indirect question.

     Mother asked if there was any milk on the doorstep.

8 Exclamation mark

This mark is used at the end of a sentence when a strong feeling is present.

A single exclamation is enough.

9 Quotation marks

These are used in pairs to enclose direct quotations.

     He asked, 'Where is my umbrella? '

Fullstops and commas go inside the quotation marks when they directly relate to the matter quoted.

     Did he ask, 'Where is my umbrella'?

10 Apostrophe

The apostrophe is used as a mark of omission as in won't, can't or it's.

It is also used to show possession, either singular or plural.

     This is Mary's hat. (singular)

     Where are the boy's clothes? (singular)

     Where are the boys' clothes? (plural; more than one boy).

Capital letters

Use an initial capital letter:

1   to begin a new sentence
2   to mark a proper noun or adjective (England, Englishman)
3   to write the days of the week and the months
4   to begin a full quotation
5   to write the names of companies, books, films, newspapers
6   to name specific courses (English Language 'O' Level)

Do not use the capital letter for general classes or names.

     Every American wants to be president.

Do not use for the seasons of the year.

Spelling

1 When you are unsure of a spelling, look up the word in a dictionary.

2 A simple jingle to remember when spelling words with 'ie' or 'ei' is:

     I before E, when sounded as E,

     Except after C

     Or when sounded as A

     As in neighbour or weigh.

3 Prefix

A prefix is one or more letters or syllables added to the beginning of a root word. When a prefix is added, the spelling of the root word remains unchanged.

     dis appear becomes **disappear**

     over worked becomes **overworked**

4 Suffix

A suffix is one or more letters or syllables added to the ending of a root word. Two rules to remember when adding suffixes are:

(a) A silent 'e' is normally dropped before adding the suffix.

bore becomes **boring**
change becomes **changing**
(b) Add a 'k' to words ending in 'c'.
picnic becomes **picnicking**
panic becomes **panicking**

Commonly misspelled words

accept (to receive)

affect (to influence)

all ready (entirely prepared)

allusion (reference)

elusion (escape)

baring (uncovering)

capital (city or letter)

complement (that which completes)

council (meeting)

dependent (when used as an adjective)

dyeing (colouring)

formally (in a formal way)

forth (forward)

licence (noun)

miner (mine worker)

personal (private)

principal (most important)

stationary (immobile)

weather (atmospheric conditions)

except (omit, excluding)

effect (result)

already (previously)

illusion (false impression)

bearing (carrying, withstanding)

capitol (building)

compliment (praise)

counsel (advice)

dependant (when used as a noun)

dying (near death)

formerly (at an earlier time)

fourth (4th)

license (verb)

minor (lesser or smaller)

personnel (staff)

principle (standard of conduct or fundamental truth)

stationery (writing supplies)

whether (conjunction)

Commonly misused words

The following pairs of words are often confused. If you are not sure of their different meanings consult a dictionary

aggravate	annoy
alternatively	alternately
anticipate	expect
appraise	apprise
appreciate	realise
appropriate	relevant
bankrupt	insolvent
biannual	biennial
comprise	compose
continuous	continual
disinterested	uninterested
eminent	imminent
enquiry	inquiry
imply	infer
learn	teach

practical	practicable
prescribe	proscribe

Some long or complex words and phrases and possible alternatives

accomplish	– do
acquaint	– tell
aquiesce	– agree
acquire	– get, gain
anticipate	– expect
approximately	– about
ascertain	– find out
come to a decision	– decide
commence	– begin, start
communicate	– write, phone
communication	– letter, postcard, phone call
consequent upon	– after
considerable	– much
considerable period	– long time
currently	– now
dearth	– lack
despatch	– send
donate	– give
due to the fact that	– because, as
endeavour	– try
experience	– feel
facilitate	– make easier
forward	– send
inform	– tell
in the course of	– during
in the event of	– if
in the meantime	– meanwhile
in the near future	– soon
locality	– place
majority	– most
materialise	– take place
on behalf of	– for
on the question of	– about
peruse	– read
proximity	– near
purchase	– buy
remunerate	– pay, reward
requirements	– needs
shall take steps to	– shall
transmit	– send
terminate	– end
utilise	– use
with regard to	– about
with the object of	– to

Appendix B Business clichés and possible alternatives

assuring you of our best attention	– [omit]
at this moment in time	– now
at your earliest convenience	– as soon as possible
be that as it may	– [omit]
enclosed herewith	– I enclose, I am enclosing
furnish particulars	– give details
hereto	– [avoid by rewording sentence]
I await the pleasure of a reply	– I look forward to hearing from you
increased consumer resistance has been encountered	– sales have dropped
inst	– [use month name instead]
of even date	– of today
ongoing	– continuing
owing to unforeseen circumstances	– unexpectedly
per	– by
re your letter	– with reference to your letter
prox	– [use month name instead]
the favour of your early reply will oblige	– I shall be glad to hear from you soon [or omit]
ult	– [use month name instead
we are desirious of	– we want
we beg to inform you	– we are writing to let you know
we take pleasure in advising	– we are pleased to let you know
your letter has come to hand	– your letter has arrived
your goodself	– you

Appendix C Writing to persons of title

Special rules apply when writing to persons of title. In the list below, each example gives the correct wording of the title (used in the address) and the conventional opening greetings and complimentary closes.

THE QUEEN

Address:	Her Majesty the Queen
Begin:	Madam
	With my humble duty
End:	I have the honour to remain (or to be)
	Madam
	Your Majesty's most humble and obedient servant

ROYAL PRINCES

Address:	His Royal Highness
	The Prince of —
Begin:	Sir
End:	I have the honour to remain (or to be)
	Sir
	Your Royal Highness's most humble and obedient servant

ROYAL PRINCESSES

Address:	Her Royal Highness
	The Princess of —
Begin:	Madam
End:	I have the honour to remain (or to be)
	Madam
	Your Royal Highness's most humble and obedient servant

DUKE

Address:	His Grace the Duke of —
Begin:	My Lord Duke
End:	Yours faithfully

DUCHESS

Address:	Her Grace the Duchess of —
Begin:	Dear Madam
End:	Yours faithfully

MARQUESS, EARL, VISCOUNT, BARON (Peers, other than a Duke)

Address:	The Most Hon the Marquess of —
	The Rt Hon the Earl of —
	The Rt Hon the Viscount —
	The Rt Hon the Lord —
Begin:	My Lord
End:	Yours faithfully

WIFE OF A PEER, OTHER THAN A DUKE

The wife of a Marquess is a MARCHIONESS
The wife of an Earl is a COUNTESS
The wife of a Viscount is a VISCOUNTESS
The wife of a Baron is a BARONESS

Address:	The Most Hon the Marchioness of —
	The Rt Hon the Countess of —
	The Rt Hon the Viscountess —
	The Rt Hon the Lady —
Begin:	Dear Madam
End:	Yours faithfully

BARONET
Address:	Sir (Christian and Surname) Bt
Begin:	Dear Sir
End:	Yours faithfully

BARONET'S WIFE
Address:	Lady (Surname only)
Begin:	Dear Madam
End:	Yours faithfully

KNIGHT
Address:	Sir (Christian and Surname) with the appropriate letters after his name
Begin:	Dear Sir
End:	Yours faithfully

KNIGHTS'S WIFE
Address:	Lady (Surname only)
Begin:	Dear Madam
End:	Yours faithfully

ARCHBISHOP
Address:	The Most Reverend the Lord Archbishop of —
Begin:	Dear Archbishop
End:	Yours sincerely

BISHOP
Address:	The Right Reverend the Lord Bishop of —
Begin:	Dear Bishop
End:	Yours sincerely

DEAN

Address: The Very Reverend the Dean of —
Begin: Dear Dean
End: Yours sincerely

ARCHDEACON

Address: The Venerable the Archdeacon of —
Begin: Dear Archdeacon
End: Yours sincerely

AMBASSADOR

Address: His Excellency (followed by any style, title or rank, and name)
Begin: Sir
End: I have the honour to be
                     Sir
                     Your Excellency's obedient servant

GOVERNOR-GENERAL or GOVERNOR

Address: His excellency
                     Name
                     Governor-General of —
                             or
                     Governor of 8 —
Begin: Sir
                     or
                     My Lord (if a peer)
End: I have the honour to be
                     Sir (My Lord, if a peer)
                     Your Excellency's obedient servant

MEMBER OF HER MAJESTY'S GOVERNMENT

Address: A letter sent to a Minister as the head of his department is addressed by his appointment only.
Begin: Dear Sir
End: Yours faithfully

If the writer knows the Minister concerned, it is permissible to write to him by his appointment, for example:

Begin: Dear Prime Minister
                     Dear Lord Privy Seal
                     Dear Chancellor
End: Yours sincerely

LORD MAYOR

Address: The Right Honourable the Lord Mayor of —
Begin: My Lord Mayor
End: Yours faithfully

MAYOR OF A CITY
Address: The Right Worshipful the Mayor of —
Begin: Mr Mayor
End: Yours faithfully

ALDERMAN
Address: Alderman (followed by any title or rank, and name)
Begin: My Lord, Dear Sir, Dear Madam, or Dear Mr Alderman
End: Yours faithfully

COUNCILLOR
As for Alderman, substituting 'Councillor' for 'Alderman'.

MEMBER OF PARLIAMENT
As in private life, with the addition of the letters MP after the name.

Appendix D Typing correction signs

Sign in margin	Meaning	Mark in text
lc/	lower case = small letters	under letter to be altered, or solidus (/); struck through letter
cap/or UC/	upper case = capital letters	under letter to be altered, or solidus (/); struck through letter
♂	delete (take out)	struck through letter
NP or //	new paragraph	through letter or word; placed before first word of new paragraph
Stet/	let it stand, ie type the dotted words	under words struck out
Run on/	no new paragraph required. Carry straight on	
⋌	insert letter, word, or words omitted	placed where the omission occurs (matter omitted is written in margin)
( )	close up — less space	between letters or words
trs/	transpose, ie, change order of words or letters as marked	between letters or words, sometimes numbered
#	insert space	
＂＂	insert inverted commas	
⸌	insert apostrophe	
⊙	insert full stop	
,/	insert comma	
;/	insert semicolon	
⊙	insert colon	
—/	insert dash	
-/	insert hyphen	